Praise for
God and the Pandemic

This is classic N. T. Wright. It is accessible to almost anyone asking questions, and yet it manages to be demanding for those who think they know the answers. It is superbly written, utterly Bible based, and leaves one satisfied at having learned and yet wanting to know more. I read it in a sitting with pleasure, provocation and profit. Do not hesitate!

—*Justin Welby, Archbishop of Canterbury*

GOD AND THE PANDEMIC

A CHRISTIAN REFLECTION ON THE CORONAVIRUS AND ITS AFTERMATH

N. T. WRIGHT

ZONDERVAN
REFLECTIVE

ZONDERVAN REFLECTIVE

God and the Pandemic
Copyright © 2020 by Tom Wright

Requests for information should be addressed to:
Zondervan, *3900 Sparks Dr. SE, Grand Rapids, Michigan 49546*

First published in Great Britain in 2020
Society for Promoting Christian Knowledge
36 Causton Street
London SW1P 4ST
www.spck.org.uk

ISBN 978-0-310-12080-3 (softcover)

ISBN 978-0-310-12082-7 (audio)

ISBN 978-0-310-12081-0 (ebook)

Old Testament quotations are from the New Revised Standard Version of the Bible, copyright © 1989 by the Division of Christian Education of the National Council of the Churches of Christ in the USA. Used by permission. All rights reserved. New Testament quotations are from the author's own translation: The New Testament for Everyone (SPCK, 2011,2019).

Extract from 'East Coker' by T. S. Eliot, in Four Quartets. London: Faber & Faber, 2001 [1979]; Orlando, FL: Harcourt, 1943. Copyright © UK, Faber & Faber; USA, Houghton Mifflin Harcourt. Reprinted with permission from Faber & Faber and Houghton Mifflin Harcourt.

Cover Design: Micah Kandros
Interior Design: The Book Guild Ltd, Leicester

Printed in the United States of America

20 21 22 23 24 25 26 27 28 29 30 /LSC/ 15 14 13 12 11 10 9 8 7 6 5 4 3 2 1

In memory of Simon Barrington-Ward KCMG
A wise and gentle saint
Bishop of Coventry 1985–1997
Died of Covid-19, Holy Saturday, April 11, 2020

Contents

N. T. Wright is research professor of New Testament and early Christianity at the University of St Andrews and senior research fellow at Wycliffe Hall, Oxford. Prior to that he was Bishop of Durham (2003–10), Canon Theologian of Westminster (2000–3), Dean of Lichfield (1994–99) and fellow, tutor, and chaplain of Worcester College, Oxford (1986–93).

Professor Wright is the author of over eighty books, including *The New Testament and the People of God* (1992), *Jesus and the Victory of God* (1994), *The Resurrection of the Son of God* (2003), *Scripture and the Authority of God* (2005), *Surprised by Hope* (2007), *Virtue Reborn* (2010), *How God Became King* (2012), *Paul and the Faithfulness of God* (2013), *The Day the Revolution Began* (2016), *Paul: A Biography* (2018) and (with Michael F. Bird) *The New Testament in Its World* (2019).

Preface and Acknowledgements

This little book would not have been written had it not been for the invitation from *TIME Magazine* to write a short piece, early on in the COVID-19 pandemic. My thanks to Belinda Luscombe for commissioning and editing that piece, and to the many who wrote to me afterwards, mostly to thank me, some to rebuke me. The present discussion is a further attempt to tease out what may wisely and biblically be said at such a time as this. As the weeks of lockdown have gone on, I, like I suppose most people, have gone through a range of emotions about it all; but it seems to me important to keep our reactions within a biblical limit, and this is what I'm trying to do here.

The aim of this book, then, is not to offer 'solutions' to the questions raised by the pandemic, to give any sort of complete analysis of what we might learn from it, or what we ought now to do. My main argument is precisely that we need to resist the knee-jerk reactions that come so readily to mind. Before we can answer those questions in anything other than the broadest outline, we need a time of lament, of restraint, of precisely not jumping to 'solutions'. These may come, God willing, but unless we retreat from our instant reactions we may not be able to hear them. If we spend time in the prayer of lament, new light may come, rather than simply the repetition of things we might have wanted to say anyway.

I am very grateful to Philip Law and his colleagues at SPCK for their willingness to take this project on at short notice, and to the old friends who have read drafts and made comments, some quite trenchant. I think particularly of Michael Lloyd,

Brian Walsh, Carey Newman, Simon Kingston, Peter Rodgers and James Ernest; and also my daughter Hattie. They are not, of course, responsible for anything that I have said. Nor is my beloved wife Maggie, whose enjoyment of the original *TIME* article provided me with encouragement to press ahead but didn't stop her from giving me pointed critique of successive drafts.

Tom Wright
Wycliffe Hall, Oxford
April 2020

I
Where Do We Start?

It sounds like one of those Greek irregular verbs: *panic, pandemic, pangolin, pandemonium*. Instead, it turns out to be an irregular virus. We'd had them before (SARS and even Mad Cow Disease). They were worrying for a time, but we got over them. Gloomy forecasts of millions of deaths turned out to be exaggerated. Surely this one would be the same?

I was reminded of the ironic quote from Pastor Martin Niemöller. There are several versions of what he may have said, but the point is the same. Speaking about 1930s Germany, he said:

> First they came for the Jews; but I did nothing because I am not a Jew. Then they came for the socialists, but I did nothing because I am not a socialist. Then they came for the Catholics, but I did nothing because I am not a Catholic. Finally, they came for me, but by then there was no-one left to help me.

So it has been, I thought, with the British and American reaction to the coronavirus. First it hit the Chinese, but we aren't Chinese, and anyway China is far away and strange things (like eating pangolins) happen there. Then it hit Iran, but we didn't worry because Iran, too, is far away, and anyway it's such a very different place. Then it struck Italy, but we thought, Well, the Italians are sociable, tactile people, of course it will spread there, but we'll be all right. And then it arrived in London. And New York... And suddenly there was no safe space on the planet.

There is no neutral zone. No medical equivalent of wartime Switzerland, where you could escape for a while, relax, and ponder what ought to be done.

So does anybody know what's going on? Why is this happening? Is someone trying to tell us something? What are we supposed to do about it?

In most of the ancient world, and many parts of the modern world too, major disasters (earthquakes, volcanoes, fires, plagues) are regularly associated with angry gods. Something bad has happened? Must be because 'someone' has it in for you. In the old pagan world of Greece and Rome, the assumption was that you hadn't offered the right sacrifices; or you hadn't said the right prayers; or you did something so truly dreadful that even the old amoral gods on Mount Olympus felt it was time to crack down on you.

The high-minded philosophers didn't think much of that. They came up with three alternatives.

First, the Stoics. Everything is programmed to turn out the way it does. You can't change it; just learn to fit in.

Alternatively, the Epicureans. Everything is random. You can't do anything about it. Make yourself as comfortable as you can.

Then the Platonists. The present life is just a shadow of reality. Bad things happen here but we are destined for a different world.

We have our modern equivalents.

Some just want to tough it out. If the bullet's got your name on it, so be it.

Most of the modern West is implicitly Epicurean. Stuff

2

happens, but we want to scramble for comfort, so settle down, self-isolate, plenty of Netflix. This too will pass.

Some – including some Christians – opt for Plato. Death isn't the worst that can happen. We're heading somewhere else anyway. All right, let's be sensible, but please don't shut down the churches. Or the golf clubs.

Meanwhile, in the refugee camps, in the multi-storey tower-blocks, in the slums and the souks, the suffering gets worse. And the sorrow rises from the whole world like a pall of smoke, shaping the question we hardly dare ask: Why?

Actually, the best answer I've heard in the last few weeks has not been to the question 'Why?' It's been to the question, 'What?' What can we do? In the UK, the government asked for volunteers to help the National Health Service with all the extra urgent non-specialist tasks. Half a million people signed up almost at once – so many that it was hard to find appropriate tasks for all of them. Retired doctors and nurses have come back into the front line. Some have themselves caught the virus and died.

They are doing what the early Christians did in times of plague. In the first few centuries of our era, when serious sickness would strike a town or city, the well-to-do would run for the hills (part of the problem was often low-lying, foetid air in a town). The Christians would stay and nurse people. Sometimes they caught the disease and died. People were astonished. What was that about? Oh, they replied, we are followers of this man Jesus. He put his life on the line to save us. So that's what we do as well.

Nobody had ever thought of doing that kind of thing before. No wonder the Gospel spread. Even when the Romans were doing their best to stamp it out.

The fascinating thing is that much of the world has picked up the hint. As the historian Tom Holland has argued in his recent book *Dominion*, much of what we take for granted in social attitudes now was Christian innovation. The ancient pagans didn't do it like that. Medicine cost money. So did education. And the poor were poor (so people assumed) because they were lazy or unlucky. It wasn't society's job to look after them.

The Christians disagreed. They picked up their rule of life from the Jews, via Jesus of course. The Jews had those texts, those scriptures, which kept on circling back to the belief that there was One God who had a special concern for the poor, the sick, the outcast, the slaves. Their thinkers sometimes flirted with bits of Stoicism or Platonism (never Epicureanism – that was a dirty word to them then, and it still is). Yet their communities, by and large, practiced a kind of extended communal family life. The early Jesus-followers got hold of that, but extended it to the increasing, and increasingly diverse, 'family' of believers. Then – long story short – the modern world, touchingly, has borrowed bits of it (medicine, education and social care for all), and sometimes thinks it has discovered this for itself, so the 'religious' bit can now drop away. Some have argued this enthusiastically, such as the Harvard psychologist Stephen Pinker.

So where do we start?

A Christian Response?

Faced with the rapid spread of the coronavirus, many people in churches have reached for 'Christian' equivalents of the ancient knee-jerk reactions. The world is full of conspiracy theories anyway: some in America think it's all China's fault, some in

China have said it's all America's fault, and no doubt there are a thousand other ideas running around, spreading themselves as easily as the virus itself and in some ways just as dangerously. The blame game is easy – especially when it's always someone *else's* fault. Those who have become accustomed to seeing all issues in terms of today's low-grade but powerful 'culture wars' will simply go for easy answers that reflect that irrelevant stand-off. The COVID-19 crisis has, in fact, done to the whole world what Hurricane Katrina did in 2005 for New Orleans: in its devastating impact, it shows that the political and social timbers have already been rotting away.

And then there are specifically (would-be) 'Christian' conspiracy theories. Some people think they know exactly what's gone wrong and what God is trying to say through it all.

Some are saying, eagerly, that this is the sign of the End. The 'End-Times' industry has been massive in America over the last couple of generations. Spin-off versions are popular in most other countries, too. Former highlights include Hal Lindsey's famous *The Late Great Planet Earth*, and the *Left Behind* series by Tim LaHaye and Jerry Jenkins. They construct a horror-movie scenario out of bits and pieces of the Bible, strung together with the string of fundamentalist piety. It's basically Platonic: 'going to heaven' is the aim, leaving the world behind to its Armageddon. And now the coronavirus is hailed as the sign that it's all about to happen.

For other Christians, this is simply a way of saying: This is a moment of opportunity! Now that everybody is thinking about death rather than wondering which cupcake to buy, perhaps there will be a massive turning to God. Perhaps we can use this moment to tell our friends about Jesus and how he can take them to heaven. Perhaps this time they'll listen.

Others quote the Old Testament prophets to produce a version of the ancient pagan theories. When bad things happen, it must be God that's done it (because he's responsible for everything), so that must mean that he is angry with us for some reason. The prophet Amos comes to mind: 'Does disaster befall a city,' he asked (Amos 3.6), 'unless the Lord has done it?' Famine, blight and pestilence – all of them were meant to lead God's people to repent of their evil ways (4.6–11). But it didn't work. So now even worse things will happen. Many of the other prophets would have agreed. Some today are eagerly jumping on this bandwagon in order to vilify their pet hates: it's all the fault of those 'other' people of whose lifestyles we disapprove.

The place to begin is with the Old Testament. That's where some of the apparently key texts can be found. Of course, this raises a big question of interpretation. Can we make a straight transfer, or at least a dynamic analogy, from what some wonderful but scary people said in the eighth century BC to our muddled and frightened world in the twenty-first century AD?

2

Reading the Old Testament

Amos said that whatever God was doing, he would reveal his secrets to 'his servants the prophets' (Amos 3.7). We have had plenty of prophets telling us what those secrets were. These range from the cause-and-effect pragmatists (it's all because governments didn't prepare properly for a pandemic) to the strikingly detached moralizers (it's all because the world needs to repent of sexual sin) to valid but separate concerns (it's reminding us about the ecological crisis). We sometimes have the impression that the coronavirus is providing people with a megaphone with which to say, more loudly, what they were wanting to say anyway.

That doesn't mean that there are not significant and rather obvious lessons to be learned. On the day I was redrafting this section, I got an email out of the blue from a medical student who has been volunteering in a hospital in East Harlem, New York. He is horrified at the way the disease is rampant among those who, unable for various reasons to get insurance, are already in bad shape from other ailments and thus likely not only to catch COVID-19 themselves, but to pass it on. This is hard-headed, feet-on-the-ground analysis of what's actually going on, not the sideways moralistic leap ('Bad things happening?' Say some people, 'That's because of abortion/gay rights/whatever'). Not a good way to go. And behind it all there are, no doubt, larger questions of geopolitics. Why did China try to muzzle reports from the World Health Organization? Why did Iran catch the disease so early? What effect did Britain's concentration on Brexit have on health policies? Actions have consequences. So does inaction.

In the Hebrew scriptures, the greatest disaster of all was the Babylonian exile. And the great prophets interpreted that event in terms of the large-scale punishment for Israel's sin. This goes back to the covenant promises and warnings – the blessings and the curses – in Deuteronomy. Books like Jeremiah and Ezekiel made it shockingly clear: Israel had done what Deuteronomy said they shouldn't (particularly, worshipping pagan idols and the behaviour that goes with that), and God had done what God said he would do in consequence. The book called Lamentations, one of the most moving long poems ever written, looks out upon a city from which people have vanished. That image haunts me now, every time I cycle around the empty streets of Oxford, normally filled with students and tourists. And the prophet weeps for the innocent children, crying for food and finding none:

> The tongue of the infant sticks to the roof of its mouth
>   for thirst;
> The children beg for food, but no one gives them
>   anything.
>
> (Lamentations 4.3; see 2.12)

Memory of the people's ancient traditions of faith only makes matters worse:

> But you, O Lord, reign for ever; your throne endures to
>   all generations.

Why have you forgotten us completely? Why have you
    forsaken us these many days?
Restore us to yourself, O Lord, that we may be restored;
    renew our days as of old—
Unless you have utterly rejected us, and are angry with
    us beyond measure.

(Lamentations 5.19–22)

The great prayers for restoration elsewhere are quite explicit:
here we are in exile because we sinned; so now we turn to you
and ask for forgiveness. Daniel 9 is perhaps the clearest:

To the Lord our God belong mercies and forgiveness, for
we have rebelled against him, and have not obeyed the
voice of the Lord our God by following his law, which he
set before us by his servants the prophets.

(Daniel 9.9–10; the whole chapter is important)

And if that's how it works on the large scale – or how it worked
with the Babylonian exile, at least – then on the smaller,
personal scale it sometimes looks as though it ought to be the
same. There's an awful moment in First Kings when a widow,
losing her only son, assumes that it's because of her sin, so that
by having the prophet Elijah staying under her roof she has
somehow triggered her son's death as a punishment (1 Kings
17.18). Elijah, raising the boy to life, puts that suggestion back
where it belongs.

But the rumour persists that ill fortune and ill behaviour are
always linked in a straightforward causal chain. The very first
Psalm informs us that good people will flourish and wicked

ones will come to a bad end. Psalm 37, which in some ways is an extended meditation on the same theme, has the striking verse:

I have been young, and now am old;
Yet I have not seen the righteous forsaken, or their
    children begging bread.

(Psalm 37.25)

Cue sharp intake of breath. We have seen them. On our streets. On our screens. On our hearts. We should probably allow the Psalmist the benefit of the doubt here: he is describing normal times. Play fair and things will work out; mess around and trouble will come. But we don't live in normal times (perhaps we never really have). What do we say then? Try explaining to someone dying of coronavirus in a crowded refugee camp that all this is because of sin. Blame the victim, in other words. That's always a popular line.

Fortunately for our sanity (and our view of biblical inspiration) there is a more rounded picture. Take Psalm 73. The writer knows the 'normal' line: good things come to good people, bad things to bad. But it hasn't worked out like that. The wicked are flourishing, and the righteous are crushed under their feet. It's only when the poet goes into God's temple that a larger, healing viewpoint can be glimpsed.

Then go to Psalm 44, which specifically denies the 'good-brings-good, bad-brings-bad' viewpoint. The poet knows that God has looked after his people in time past. But now truly horrible things have happened, despite the fact that, as he insists,

All this has come upon us, yet we have not forgotten you
    Or been false to your covenant.

Our heart has not turned back...
If we had forgotten the name of our God,
   Or spread out our hands to a strange god,
Would not God discover this?
   For he knows the secrets of the heart.
Because of you were are being killed all day long,
   And accounted as sheep for the slaughter.

                             (Psalm 44.17–22)

Paul quotes that in Romans 8, one of the most important places for understanding this whole mystery. We'll come back to that in a later chapter.

There are other Psalms which state the problem and leave it with a kind of puzzled shrug of the shoulders. Psalm 89 is like that. God has made wonderful promises; we basked in their sunshine for a while; but now the sky is dark and everything has gone wrong and there is no hope in sight. End of Psalm. There's a refreshing honesty to that.

Or – the darkest spot of all – there is Psalm 88. Once when my wife and I were leading a pilgrimage to the Holy Land we got to the place where, according to some of the archaeologists, Jesus probably spent the last night before his crucifixion. It was a dungeon deep below the palace of the first-century High Priest. Our guide suggested we pause and read Psalm 88. It was perfect, and perfectly harrowing:

My soul is full of troubles, and my life draws near
   to Sheol.
I am counted among those who go down to the Pit,
   I am like those who have no help, like those forsaken
   among the dead, like the slain that lie in the grave...

O Lord, why do you cast me off? Why do you hide your
   face from me? Wretched and close to death from my
   youth up, I suffer your terrors; I am desperate...
You have caused friend and neighbour to shun me;
   my companions are in darkness.

(Psalm 88.3–5, 14–15, 18)

Those Psalms are the foothills, already gloomy and frightening.
Yet we sense a darker mountain looming up behind them.
It's called the Book of Job. Whenever anyone tells you that
coronavirus means that God is calling people – perhaps you!
– to repent, tell them to read Job. The whole point is that *that
is not the point*.

It is Job's 'comforters' who tell him it's all about sin. They are
absolutely clear that God must be punishing Job for some secret
misbehaviour. Job is equally clear that if that is so then God is
being unjust. The reader, in on the secret from the start, knows
that both are wrong, but that the 'comforters' are a whole lot
more wrong than Job. Quite a different battle is going on. The
book of Job rattles the cages of our easy-going piety. It reminds
us that there are indeed more things in heaven and earth – more
pains and puzzles in heaven and earth – than are dreamed of in
our philosophy. Even our 'Christian' philosophy.

The book of Job doesn't really have a 'resolution'. Not a
satisfactory one. There is a short 'happy ending', but it's only
partially happy: Job gets more sons and daughters to replace the
ones he lost, but does that make it all right? God has revealed
his power and might to Job, and Job realizes he can't compete;
but does even that make it all right? That might conceivably just
leave you with the Stoics: It's all fixed, you can't do anything,
you might as well put up with it.

I think part of the point of Job is precisely its unresolved character. Sermons have been preached, and whole books written, on the ways in which the story of Jesus provides a kind of resolution for Job. Well, maybe. Job longs for someone to stand in the middle, between him and God, so that the case could be heard, so that both sides could be represented. There is no umpire between us, he complains, who might lay his hand on us both (9.33). He questions whether mortals can live again, after they die (14.14). He longs for ultimate justice, a putting-right of things which goes way beyond what this life seems to afford (21, 23–24). All of these things are spoken of in the New Testament in connection with what the same God, Israel's God, has done and will do through Jesus. Jesus stands between God and humans. He has shown the way through death to renewed life. He has put all things right, and will work that out in the end.

Yet this is anything but straightforward. The book of Job is a standing reminder that the Old Testament operates on at least two quite different levels. There is the story of Israel – or rather, of God-and-Israel. This is the covenantal story: the narrative of how the Creator God called a people to be his partner in rescuing the human race and restoring creation. It tells of how that people – themselves 'carriers' of the disease that had infected the whole human race, the proto-virus called 'idolatry and injustice' which is killing us all – how that people themselves had to go into the darkness of exile so that, somehow, new life might emerge the other side.

That whole story, seen with hindsight by the followers of Jesus, has its own dynamic. Many Jews in Jesus' day were very much aware of the great story of God and Israel in terms of the 'covenant' in Deuteronomy 27–32, which promised blessings for obedience and curses – ultimately, exile – for disobedience, followed in the end by a restoration when Israel finally repented and turned back to God. This story is picked up in the great prayer of Daniel 9. The extraordinary poem we know as Isaiah 40–55 tells the same story, of God's healing, rescue, restoration and new creation following after a time not only of judgment but even of despair. Seen from the perspective of a first-century Jew, these scriptural traditions all belonged together. Jesus and his first followers drew liberally on that whole story to explain what was now happening.

Alongside this Israel-and-God story there runs the deeper story of the good creation and the dark power that from the start has tried to destroy God's good handiwork. I do not claim to understand that dark power. As I shall suggest later, I don't think we're meant to. We are simply to know that when we are caught up in awful circumstances, apparent gross injustices, terrible plagues – or when we are accused of wicked things of which we are innocent, suffering strange sicknesses with no apparent reason, let alone cure – at those points we are to lament, we are to complain, we are to state the case, and leave it with God. God himself declares at the end that Job has told the truth (42.8). He has clung on to the fact that God is just, even though his own misery seems to deny it.

Jesus not only drew on that story. He lived it. He died under it.

That brings us, then, to the story of Jesus himself.

3
Jesus and the Gospels

One of the great New Testament words is *Now*. That was then, this is now. *But now*, says St Paul, moving from his analysis of human plight to his exposition of God's solution (Romans 3.21). Something new is happening. 'The time is fulfilled,' said Jesus; and his hearers, conscious of living within the perplexing story of Israel's scriptures, picked up at least that something long-awaited was now arriving. Or at least that Jesus thought it was. Jesus, like the ancient prophets before him whom he quoted, was announcing – yes! – that people should repent. Well of course; isn't that what prophets are supposed to do?

Yes and no. Jesus could on occasion point to disasters that had happened and warn his hearers that unless they repented they would be next (Luke 13.1–9). Yet that was very specific: the Roman governor had sent in the troops and killed pilgrims in the temple, and then a nearby tower had collapsed and crushed eighteen people to death. Were they worse sinners than all the others in Jerusalem? No, says Jesus: 'Unless you repent, you will all be destroyed in the same way.' This was a particular moment, the decisive moment in fact for the history of ancient Israel, of the Jewish people and institutions of the time. The warnings were all about the imminent destruction of Jerusalem. Unless the people changed their ways radically, then Roman swords and falling stonework would finish most of them off. Jesus could read 'the signs of the times' even if most of his contemporaries couldn't (Luke 12.49–59). So far, so prophetic. Forty years later, Jesus was proved right.

Yet Jesus went further. When people asked him for 'a sign from heaven', he saw their request as a sign of unbelief. They wanted things to be obvious. The only sign he would give them, he said, was another prophetic sign: the sign of Jonah (Matthew 12.39). Jonah disappeared into the belly of the whale – and then came out alive, three days later. That, said Jesus, was the 'sign' that would tell his generation what was going on. The other 'signs' that Jesus was doing were not negative ones. They were not like the prophetic 'signs' to which Amos referred, or indeed like the 'signs' that Moses and Aaron performed in Egypt to try to shake Pharaoh out of his complacency and allow the Israelites to go free. Those 'signs' were strange warning signals: plagues of frogs, or locusts, or rivers turning into blood. Jesus' 'signs' (John gives us a neat catalogue of them) were all about new creation: water into wine, healings, food for the hungry, sight for the blind, life for the dead. The other Gospels chip in with several more, including parties with all the wrong kind of people, indicating a future full of forgiveness. All these were forward-looking signs, declaring the new thing that God was doing. Was doing *now*.

So Jesus seems to have been standing at the threshold. Sometimes he could speak and act like an Old Testament prophet – and people did say that he reminded them of Jeremiah or Elijah, which gives you rather a different picture to the standard image of Jesus 'meek and mild'. On another occasion, after healing a man, he warns him, 'Don't sin anymore, in case something worse happens' (John 5.14). Yet at other times he seems to have been looking, not backward to sins which might bring about judgment, but forward to the new thing that was happening: the kingdom of God.

That is certainly the picture we get from John 9. Jesus and his disciples come upon a man who had been blind from birth. His disciples ask the standard question, not that different from the question many people are asking today about the coronavirus:

> Teacher, whose sin was it that caused this man to be born blind? Did he sin, or did his parents?

Jesus' answer puts paid to any easy-going vending-machine theology (one sin in, one punishment out).

> 'He didn't sin,' replied Jesus, 'nor did his parents. It happened so that God's works could be seen in him.'
>
> (John 9.1–3)

Jesus, in other words, doesn't look *back* to a hypothetical *cause* which would enable the onlookers to feel smug that they had understood some inner cosmic moral mechanism, some sin that God had had to punish. He looks *forward* to see *what God is going to do about it*. That translates directly into what *he*, Jesus, is going to do about it. For he is the light of the world.

So he heals the man. This is the *now* time. Not the time for speculating about previous sin.

Jesus Himself Is the Ultimate "Sign"

We have seen how the Gospels present Jesus as standing at a moment of great transition. He is summing up the whole ancient prophetic tradition and re-expressing its message in terms of the last great warning to Jerusalem and its inhabitants. Turn now, he says, follow God's way of peace rather than your

crazy flight into national rebellion against Rome. If you don't,
it will mean disaster. This becomes perhaps most explicit in
Luke 19, as Jesus rides into Jerusalem on a donkey – in tears,
lamenting the destruction that will come on the city because
the people had indeed refused his way of peace.

At the same time, Jesus is pointing forwards to a new world,
a world in which he himself will be the one true sign: pointing
– like Jonah's symbolic 'death and resurrection' – to the
worldwide call to repent. When he does talk of wars, famines,
earthquakes and the like he doesn't say 'So when these things
happen you must think carefully about what you and your
society should be repenting of'. He says 'Don't be disturbed;
the end is not yet' (Matt. 24.6). If people had paid attention
to that, we should have had less alarmist teaching about 'the
End-Times', whether the Hal Lindsay variety, the LaHaye and
Jenkins kind, or the present new wave. Conspiracy theories
were thriving in the first century, just as they are today. Jesus
pushes them aside. Stay calm, he says, and trust in me.

In particular – it is remarkable how little this gets noticed –
Jesus gave his followers a prayer, which more or less all Christian
traditions use to this day, and which anchors the key prophetic
points in the now of the Gospel. In this 'Lord's Prayer' Jesus-
followers pray, not just when a sudden global crisis occurs, but
every single day, 'Thy kingdom come, on earth as in heaven'.
They also pray, every day, not simply when a horrible event acts
as a trigger, 'Forgive us our trespasses'.

Being kingdom-people and being penitence-people
comes with the turf. That's part of what following Jesus is
all about. Praying those two prayers – the kingdom-prayer,
the forgiveness-prayer – might just alert us to the real anti-
kingdom forces at work in our world, our real 'trespasses'

(against one another, in our political systems; against the natural world and particularly the animal kingdom, in our farming and food-chain systems) of which we should have repented long ago.

In other words, if Jesus' followers are waiting for special events to nudge them into looking for Jesus' kingdom on earth as in heaven, or to tell them to repent when they were drifting into careless sin, then they've gone to sleep on the job. That is not to say, of course, that Christians never do go to sleep on the job, or that God cannot and doesn't give them a kick or a prod from time to time to get them back on track. That, too, is taken care of in the Lord's Prayer: don't lead us into the time of testing, and deliver us from evil. In a sense, learning to follow Jesus is simply learning to pray the Lord's Prayer.

If we really do that, we will be delivered from the false 'explanations' that imagine that the kingdom will come with sudden signs (despite the fact that Jesus said it wouldn't), or that a new event, after the time of Jesus, will be a global call to repent (despite the fact that Jesus saw his own death and resurrection as the once-for-all summons). We shall discover the truth that the Letter to the Hebrews declares when it puts Jesus as the last and greatest of the prophets: God has indeed spoken of old through the prophets, but in these last days 'God has spoken through his son' (Hebrews 1.2).

This provides a vital answer to the question which lies behind a lot of the speculation and argument about how to apply the Bible to great and disturbing events of our own time. The New Testament insists that we put Jesus at the centre of the picture and work outwards from there. The minute we find ourselves looking at the world around us and jumping to conclusions about God and what he might be doing, *but without looking carefully at Jesus*, we are in serious danger of forcing through an 'interpretation' which might look attractive – it might seem quite 'spiritual' and awe-inspiring – but which actually screens Jesus out of the picture. As the old saying has it, if he is not Lord of all, he is not Lord at all.

So, what might trusting in Jesus mean in practice?

There is after all only one Jesus: the Jesus of Nazareth who came into Galilee saying *Now*. Now is the time for God to become king. Now is the time to repent and believe the good news. At every point Jesus was redefining all the ancient promises about God becoming king, about the good news that God was coming back at last to set everything right. He was redefining it all around his own vision. That's why he told 'parables' – vivid stories which said *Yes* to the kingdom of God and *No* to the ways in which most of his contemporaries were seeing that 'kingdom', that 'sovereignty', that divine 'control'.

That's not just a first-century issue, though it certainly was that too. It is vital for our own reflection. A lot of the talk about 'What is God doing in the coronavirus pandemic' assumes that God is 'sovereign', *and it assumes what that 'sovereignty' will mean*. Jesus, though, was unveiling a different meaning of divine sovereignty. *This is what it looks like*, he was saying as he healed a leper, or as he announced forgiveness on his own authority to a penitent woman. *This is what it looks like*, he was saying as he celebrated parties with all the wrong people. *This is what it looks like*, he was saying as he went up to Jerusalem that last time and solemnly announced God's final judgment on the city, the system, and the institution – the Temple – that had refused God's way of peace. *This is what it looks like*, he said as he broke bread on the last night with his friends. *This is what it looks like*, he said as he hung on the cross, with the words 'King of the Jews' above his head.

This is what it looks like, he was saying three days later to his astonished friends in the upper room.

Unless we are prepared to see these events – the Jesus-events, the messianic moment – as the ultimate call to penitence, because they are the ultimate announcement of the arrival of God's kingdom, we will be bound to over-interpret other events to compensate. There will be a vacuum, a Jesus-shaped blank, and we shall fill it by saying (as Jesus had warned that people would say) 'Look here!' or 'Look there!' (Luke 17.21)

For Jesus' first followers, then, his death and resurrection were now the single, ultimate 'sign'. Prophets like Amos had been forerunners. God has now spoken through the Son, once and for all. For us to try to read God's secret code off the pages of the newspapers may look clever. We may even get a reputation for spiritual insight – but actually, we are doing it because we have forgotten where the true key to understanding is now to be found.

Similarly, any claim to tell from world events when the 'second coming' will occur is a claim to know more than Jesus himself (Mark 13.32). Jesus himself is the reason why people should turn from idolatry, injustice and all wickedness. The cross is where all the world's sufferings and horrors have been heaped up and dealt with. The resurrection is the launch of God's new creation, of his sovereign saving rule on earth – starting with the physical body of Jesus himself. Those events are now *the* summons to repent and *the* clue to what God is doing in the world. Trying to jump from an earthquake, a tsunami, a pandemic or anything else to a conclusion about 'what God is saying here' without going through the Gospel story is to make the basic theological mistake of trying to deduce something about God while going behind Jesus' back.

You can see the same point in Jesus' story about the vineyard tenants (Mark 12.1–12, with parallels in Matthew and Luke). The story is well known: the vineyard owner sends messengers to get fruit, and the tenants reject them and even kill some of them. Finally the owner plays his last possible card: he sends his only son. Surely, he thinks, they will respect him. But they don't. They kill him, too, and throw his body out. *After that there can be no more messengers*. The application is obvious. Jesus is saying, No more warning signs after this.

The historical point here is that once God's people have rejected him, they have blown their last chance to avoid the destruction that Jesus had warned would come upon the nation and particularly the Temple. Yet the point applies equally as the Church moves forwards. What was said about the One God sending his only son to the vineyard tenants – to the people of Israel – was then applied to the Church's mission to the world. If there is One God, and if he has come in the person of his own son to unveil his rescuing purposes for the world, then there can be no other signs, no other warning events, to compare with this one.

Of course, again, God can do whatever God wants. If he wants to draw things to people's attention in a special way, that is up to him. (The day I wrote this I was cleaning up in the kitchen and stood up suddenly, crashing my head into a cupboard door. As I picked myself up from the floor I wondered whether God was saying something to me. My only conclusion was that I was trying to do too many things at once.) But this is not the norm. It is not what we should expect. We are not to be like horses and mules, without understanding, needing to be prodded and yanked by bits and bridles (Psalm 32.9). From now on, the summons to repentance, and the announcement of God's kingdom on earth as in heaven, come not through wars, earthquakes, famines or plagues. (Or domestic accidents.) They come through Jesus. Through the story of Jesus himself, told, preached, announced; through the people of Jesus, the people in whose lives Jesus himself lives by his Spirit; through the strange work of Jesus even in parts of the world where his name is not recognized. If God wants to alert us to things that are wrong in the way we have been running the world – and that seems to me highly likely – they will come to us Jesus-shaped. Jesus' announcement of God's kingdom is the gold standard. There is a good reason why the reading of a passage from the Gospels is a compulsory part of all traditional repetitions of Jesus' Last Supper. These are the words of life – which therefore contain also the words of warning. There are not going to be any more 'final messengers'.

When we talk about God's coming kingdom, and about it being inaugurated already through the work of Jesus, it may be worth reminding ourselves what this actually means. So much misinformation on this subject has leaked into Christianity over the last few hundred years that it's sometimes hard to get things straight. When we talk about 'the kingdom of God', or God's ultimate future, from whatever angle, the New Testament insists that this is not a matter of saved souls 'going to heaven' and leaving 'earth' behind for good. I have set all this out in *Surprised by Hope* (2007), and it has considerable bearing on what we are saying now.

Paul speaks glowingly in Ephesians 1.10 of God's ultimate plan being to sum up everything in the Messiah, things in heaven and things on earth. The Platonic dream, so popular in much Christian piety (particularly when faced with a rampant secular culture that appears to have taken over the 'earth'), is simply escapist. In fact, the modern myth that the early Christians expected 'the end of the world' very soon is a straightforward misreading of the relevant first-century texts. Jesus insisted that God's kingdom – God's sovereign, saving rule on earth as in heaven – was being inaugurated through him and his work, and that 'some standing here' wouldn't die until they had seen it happening 'in power' (Mark 9.1).

So when did that happen? According to Jesus himself, 'All authority in heaven and on earth has been given to me' (Matthew 28.18). Not *will* be given; *has been* given. According to Paul, summing up the Gospel message at the start of his greatest letter, Jesus 'was marked out powerfully as God's son in terms of the spirit of holiness by the resurrection of the dead' (Rom. 1.4). This means – contrary to much popular imagination, both Christian and non-Christian – that Jesus is already reigning. Paul speaks in First Corinthians of Jesus' *present* rule over the world, starting with his resurrection and ending when he has finished the work of subduing all 'enemies' – the last of which is death itself, a very relevant consideration at this time (1 Corin. 15.25–26).

So how do the Gospels describe the Jesus who thus embodies the renewed and rescuing sovereignty of God? What is this 'rule' supposed now to look like? Here we encounter the thing which makes the Christian message so distinctive, and which must colour all our attempts to understand or interpret current events.

We all know, of course, that Jesus died by crucifixion, and well-taught Christians have developed various ways of spelling out the early claim that 'he died for our sins'. Rather fewer, however, have followed up the central Gospel insight which is symbolized in the 'title' on the cross – 'King of the Jews' in Hebrew, Greek and Latin. Jesus himself, in several sayings, saw his forthcoming death not only as 'salvific' in the traditional sense of 'saving souls', but as 'kingdom-bringing'. When faced with two of his right-hand men, James and John, wanting the best seats 'in the kingdom', Jesus responded by redefining power itself. The world's rulers exercise power by bossing and bullying, he said; but we're going to do it the other way. The greatest must be the servant. The one who wants to be first must be slave of all. Then comes the crunch: he explains that this is so *because* the son of man didn't come to be served, but to serve, and to give his life as a ransom for many (Mark 10.45).

Jesus' own unique saving vocation has thus redefined power and authority for all time. What most of the western Christian tradition has managed to ignore – because it has separated out 'salvation' on the one hand from 'power' on the other, as though the two were not intimately related! – is that the 'atonement' theology of that punch-line comes *within* the redefinition of 'power', and vice versa. The secret of God's saving power is the self-giving love of the incarnate Son.

The point is this. *If you want to know what it means to talk about God being 'in charge of' the world, or being 'in control', or being 'sovereign', then Jesus himself instructs you to rethink the notion of 'kingdom', 'control' and 'sovereignty' themselves, around his death on the cross.*

We can focus this insight on one of the most poignant passages in the Gospels. In John 11, Jesus and his followers head back towards Jerusalem, despite, or even perhaps because of, the strong suspicion that an evil fate is waiting for him there. They come to Bethany. Word has already reached them that their friend Lazarus, who was particularly dear to Jesus, has been sick; then, soon after, that he had died. John's reader will already be wondering: why could not Jesus, who healed a stranger's son at a distance (John 5.43–54), not have done the same for his friend?

This is the point, however, when we begin (with fear and trembling) to see what it might mean to be a friend of Jesus. John invites us to read between the lines. When, eventually, Jesus gives the command to take away the stone from the tomb so that he can call Lazarus out and back into life, the first thing he does is to pray with thanksgiving that God had heard his prayer. This must mean that, before journeying to Bethany, Jesus had prayed that Lazarus, though dead, would not decompose, and would be ready to be raised back to life. The stone is taken away; Martha's fears of a rotting smell are not realized (John doesn't say that, but he leaves us to figure it out). Jesus knows that the road is now clear. He remains sovereign through all of this; sovereign in knowing what is going on, what it will cost the family to go through this terrible moment, and what he will then do. This is all part of the dark mystery which John is unveiling, the mystery in which Jesus himself will shortly go down into death in order to overthrow 'the ruler of this world' (12.31), and, unlike Lazarus in this incident, will emerge into a new kind of life, and immortal physicality, the other side. (Note that Lazarus comes out of the tomb still wrapped up in the grave-clothes. Jesus, in John 20, has left his behind.)

So here is the paradox, which I suggest as a vital clue for how we should approach the whole question of understanding our present predicament. The Jesus who has prayed, who is taking charge, who knows what he is going to do – this Jesus *weeps at the tomb of his friend* (John 11.35). It would be ridiculous to suggest (as one can imagine some nervous theologians suggesting) that he was just putting on a show of emotion in order to demonstrate sympathy with Mary and Martha. No: the tears are real. The horror of death – the fact that it sneers in the face of all that is lovely and beautiful – is overwhelming, even for the Lord of life. Especially for the Lord of life. And the tears of Jesus at the tomb of Lazarus point on to 'now is my soul troubled' in 12.27, to Mark's and Matthew's description of Jesus in Gethsemane, and to the awful 'My God, why did you abandon me' on the cross itself (Matthew 12.46; Mark 15.34). That sequence – which could of course be filled out in considerable detail – adds up to the complex ways in which the different Gospels understand the very notion of power itself, of divine 'control' or 'taking charge', the central idea of 'kingdom', being redefined around Jesus.

Come back to the tomb of Lazarus, with our present coronavirus questions ringing in our heads. Martha and Mary, and then the bystanders, both say in effect that it's Jesus's fault. He could have done something to stop this. 'Lord, if only you'd been here, my brother wouldn't have died!' (John 11.21, 32). 'Couldn't he have done something?' ask the crowd (11.37). The question echoes down the years, with every new tragedy. Why did God allow this? Why didn't God step in and stop it?

As with the man born blind, Jesus isn't looking back to see what might or might not have happened. People have blamed him, but he isn't going to blame anyone. He has trusted his Father, and is looking ahead to see what must now happen. And the way to that goal is through tears. The God who John has told us became incarnate in and as Jesus of Nazareth is the God, the Word-Made-Flesh, who weeps at the tomb of his friend.

That could be the clue to a great deal of wisdom. Wisdom that we need rather badly right now.[1]

So how is Jesus to engage with Martha, Mary and the critical crowd? He doesn't turn the tables on them and suggest that all this happened because they were sinful and now ought to repent. He just weeps. And then – with the authority born of that mixture of tears and trust – he commands Lazarus to come out of the tomb. If there is a word for our present situation, facing not only a pandemic but all the consequent social and cultural upheaval, I think it might be right here.

What, then, have we learned so far?

First, we've leaned how Jesus redefines what it means to say that God is in control, that God is taking charge. We in the modern West have split apart the doctrines of providence (God's overall supervision of everything that happens) and atonement (God's forgiveness of our sins through the death of Jesus). The New Testament refuses to do that. *Jesus himself* refused to do that. But this habit of mind has become so engrained that it is possible for theologians and popular Christian writers to talk about what we might or might not say about a major pandemic on one side of the room, as it were, and to assume on the other side of the room that this provides an occasion for us to say that Jesus died for our sins so that we could go to heaven if we trust him. The New Testament knows nothing of a room with those two separate sides. Somehow we have to learn to put back together what should never have been split apart.

Second, as Jesus brings to a peak the Old Testament prophetic tradition, so he rounds it off by drawing the full significance of

---

1   A similar claim is also made, from a fascinatingly complementary angle, by the Japanese artist Makoto Fujimura in his new book *Theology of Making* (Yale University Press, 2020).

it all on to himself and his forthcoming death and resurrection. No doubt, thereafter, God can and does use all kinds of events to alert us to things we need to see but might ignore. Yet when that happens, we should not interpret them behind the back of the incarnate Son. In the normal course of events, we should assume that the 'sign' par excellence of all that the One God has done, is doing and will do is Jesus himself, Jesus the Messiah of Israel, Jesus crucified, risen, ascended, promising to return in glory; Jesus the true Lord of the world.

So what does it look like to 'read' the events in the world in the light of Jesus' death and resurrection? For that we pass to the rest of the New Testament.

4

Reading the New Testament

The New Testament refers back constantly, as do more or less all Jewish writings, to the great foundational events of Passover, the time when God rescued Israel from slavery in Egypt. Jesus himself made Passover central to his work of announcing God's kingdom, and to his vocation to go to the cross. That is why he chose Passover to go to Jerusalem that last time, and why, in order to interpret his death beforehand, he gave his followers a meal which both belongs with Passover itself and which points forward to what he was to accomplish the next day.

Now the thing about Passover – one of the things about Passover! – is that when Israel was enslaved in Egypt *nobody ever said it was as a result of their sin*. To be sure, in Jesus' time, the terrible situation of the Jewish people (having been trampled on by Babylon, Greece, Syria and now Rome) meant that they regularly interpreted their plight not just in terms of needing a 'new Exodus', but also in terms of needing the 'forgiveness of sins' that Isaiah and the other prophets had promised. Exile was undoubtedly (from the prophets' point of view) the result of sin, so rescue from exile would mean forgiveness. Yet Passover was never about forgiveness. Jacob and his sons were hardly paragons of virtue, but Genesis makes no connection between that and the long years of slavery. Indeed, when the famine strikes the Middle East, they don't say 'Ah, this is because we've sinned'. They say, 'We've heard there is corn in Egypt.' They are not looking backwards at what might have caused the problem. They are looking forward to see what needs to be done.

That sets the pattern for one of the first, and most interesting, examples from the early days of the Church. A pattern that could point forwards to our own appropriate response to our present problems.

The early chapters of the book of Acts paint a vivid picture of the life of the early Church. It's quite a page-turner, and in the midst of the comings and goings and some dramatic moments it might be easy to miss an incident full of significance in itself and for our particular theme. Acts 11 takes us to the church in Syrian Antioch, roughly three hundred miles north of Jerusalem. It's a bustling, cosmopolitan city, right on the trade routes, with people from any and every country either resident or passing through. Many people – from many different nationalities – have come to believe in Jesus, and the Church is growing. Barnabas comes from Jerusalem to check it out and is delighted, because he can see God's grace so clearly at work (11.23). Then Barnabas goes to find Saul (who becomes 'Paul' not long after this) and brings him to help with the work of teaching and preaching.

It was around this time that travelling prophets arrived in Antioch from Jerusalem. One of them, named Agabus, stood up and told the assembly what the Spirit had revealed to him. There would, he announced, be a great famine over the whole world. These things happened from time to time, as they had done nearly two millennia earlier, bringing Jacob and his family to Egypt. Luke comments that the famine actually took place in the reign of Claudius (i.e. AD 41–54). We know from other historical sources of more than one serious famine in that period.

So what do the Antioch Jesus-followers say? They do *not* say either 'This must be a sign that the Lord is coming back soon!'

or 'This must mean that we have sinned and need to repent' – or even 'this will give us a great opportunity to tell the wider world that everyone has sinned and needs to repent'. Nor do they start a blame-game, looking around at the civic authorities in Syria, or the wider region, or even the Roman empire, to see whose ill-treatment of the eco-system, or whose tampering with food distribution networks, might have contributed to this dangerous situation. They ask three simple questions: Who is going to be at special risk when this happens? What can we do to help? And who shall we send?

Some might look at this and think, Well, that's pretty untheological as a response. It's just pragmatic. But that would actually be the really 'untheological' response. Here we stumble upon one of the great principles of the kingdom of God – the principle that God's kingdom, inaugurated through Jesus, is all about restoring creation the way it was meant to be. *God always wanted to work in his world through loyal human beings.* That is part of the point of being made 'in God's image'. So, just as when in John 9 Jesus says that the works of God are going to be revealed, and then goes to work himself, we can imagine the Antioch church figuring out prayerfully what God was doing – not why the famine was occurring but what was to be done to help – and realizing that *what God was doing, he was going to do through them.* That is part of believing in the work of the Holy Spirit. They were a busy and apparently prosperous church; the Jerusalem church was poor and (sporadically) persecuted. So the first two questions weren't hard. Then it was just a matter of prayerfully considering who to send. This is the kind of thing that Paul has in mind, I think, when he later writes to the Roman Christians that God works *with and through those* who love him to bring all things to a good end (Rom. 8.28). We will come back to that.

(Notice, by the way, one feature of the early Church in this story. Never before in world history had a multi-cultural group in one city felt under any fraternal obligation to a mono-cultural group in another city three hundred miles away. The Jewish communities around the world would have understood the principle. Members of the Roman imperial civil service might have seen themselves as part of the same larger team as colleagues in another province. But the Church? We here witness something unprecedented. And very powerful. As we face our own questions about how to help, this example should be regularly before our eyes. Whatever the 'Christian' response to Covid-19 should be, it should be one in which all Christians can join.)

The point is that under the 'new covenant' spoken of by Jesus on the night he was betrayed – a reference to Jeremiah 31 – the early Church believed that God was energizing them by his own personal presence. The Spirit was given so that individual believers, and still more the believers when joined together for corporate worship, would take up their responsibilities as God's eyes and ears, his hands and his feet, to do what needed to be done in the world. This is why, from the very start, the early Christians looked out at the world, as Jesus had looked out upon his beloved people Israel, and had seen what God was wanting to do and say, and had prayerfully got on and done and said that themselves. That is what 'mission' is all about. As Jesus himself said in John 20.21, 'As the father has sent me, so I'm sending you.' As Jesus had been to Israel, so his followers were to be to the world. This is how it happens. And remember: Jesus said that to a small group of people who were locked in because they were afraid. Sound familiar? We'll come back to that.

After all, the programmatic statement of God's kingdom in the Sermon on the Mount (Matt. 5–7) isn't simply about 'ethics', as people often imagine in our shrunken Western world. It's about mission. 'Blessed are the poor in spirit… the meek… the mourners… the peacemakers… the hungry-for-justice people' and so on. We all too easily assume that Jesus is saying 'try hard to be like this, and if you can manage it you'll be the sort of people I want in my kingdom'. But that's not the point! The point is that *God's kingdom is being launched on earth as in heaven, and the way it will happen is by God working through people of this sort.* After all, so often when people look out on the world and its disasters they wonder, why God doesn't just march in and take over. Why, they ask, does he permit it? Why doesn't he send a thunderbolt (or perhaps something a little less like what a pagan deity might do, but still) and put things right? The answer is that God *does* send thunderbolts – human ones. He sends in the poor in Spirit, the meek, the mourners, the peacemakers, the hungry-for-justice people. They are the way God wants to act in his world. They are more effective than any lightning flashes or actual thunderbolts. They will use their initiative; they will see where the real needs are, and go to meet them. They will weep at the tombs of their friends. At the tombs of their enemies. Some of them will get hurt. Some may be killed. That is the story of Acts, all through. There will be problems, punishments, setbacks, shipwrecks, but God's purpose will come through. These people, prayerful, humble, faithful, will be the answer, not to the question Why? But to the question What? What needs to be done here? Who is most at risk? How can we help?

Who shall we send? God works in all things *with and through* those who love him.

None of this is to say that there will not be lessons to be learned in due course. It is all, in fact, pointing to the questions we must ask at the more global scale a little later. First, we move on to Paul's journeys and letters. I note in passing that when he addresses a situation in Corinth where there is some kind of a social crisis – probably another famine – he doesn't tell the Corinthians to figure out what sin they or someone else had committed. He tells them, as a bit of prudential wisdom, that right now it's better just to hold on, to see the crisis through, not to try for major life-changes. That's in 1 Corinthians 7: a controversial passage, but I think that's what's going on. Yes, there's a crisis; but no, you mustn't be alarmed. Just be wise about what you do and don't do while it's going on.

Perhaps the central point comes in Acts 17. Paul has arrived in Athens. He follows his usual pattern of speaking in the Jewish synagogues; but here he also gets out and about in the marketplace. I suspect he had been looking forward to this moment. Paul had grown up in Tarsus, which along with Athens was one of the main centres of philosophy in Paul's day. That was because, back in 86 BC, the Romans had devastated Athens in punishment for giving support to Rome's enemies in an ongoing war. Most of the philosophers had left town. Many went to Tarsus. Paul knew his philosophy.

Anyway, Paul's teaching aroused not just interest but suspicion. The ancient world was tolerant of strange new cults. People worshipped their local gods or (in the case of Athens) goddesses, but there were numerous other temples and shrines. An easy-going pluralism was normally the order of the day. However, there were limits. Famously, Socrates had fallen foul of the Athenian magistrates on that point: he had been put to death for corrupting the young (i.e. teaching them strange new ideas which might subvert the normal social order) and for introducing 'foreign divinities'. Paul was summoned to address the Court of the Areopagus, and in particular to explain just what he meant by talking about 'Jesus and Anastasis'. *Anastasis* is the Greek for 'resurrection'; they seem to have thought he was talking about a new god (Jesus) and a new goddess (Anastasis). This was not, then, primarily a philosophical discussion. It was potentially a capital charge.

In that light, what Paul does is all the more interesting. His aim is to work round to the announcement that there is One God, that this One God is going to hold the whole world to account (he is speaking, remember, to the High Court in Athens!), and that the guarantee and means of this final judgment will be the man Jesus, whom God has raised from the dead. And the whole point is that this message *constitutes a summons to repent* (Act 17.30–31).

Ah, some might think, that's what we hoped was coming. But think for a moment about what Paul does *not* do. He could have plucked a few examples of recent disasters. There had been other famines. There were major social and political struggles. He could have referred them all the way back, over a century earlier, to that awful day when Athens backed the wrong political horse and Rome, with no regard for the great past of a civilization, smashed the place up. In terms of ancient religion, all that kind of thing says 'the gods must be angry'. It looks pretty much like a summons to repent.

Yet Paul doesn't go there. He simply refers to the one great sign: God is calling all people everywhere to repent *through the events concerning Jesus*. Jesus himself is the One Great

Sign. Paul will not allow anything else to be superimposed over that. Jesus himself had warned that there could be no more warning prophets. Once the vineyard owner had sent the son, he had made the ultimate, unrepeatable offer. That is the logic underneath Paul's careful speech. He is talking (as people do today) of God's kingdom; he is talking about the need for people to repent; but the argument hinges, not on any independent events, not on some big crisis that's just occurred, but on the facts concerning Jesus himself.

I suggest, then, that from the time of Jesus onwards we see Jesus' followers telling people about God's kingdom, and summoning them to repent, not because of any subsequent events such as famines or plagues but because of Jesus himself.

One early Christian book, however, might seem to be going in the opposite direction. That is the book of Revelation, where there is a sequence of 'plagues' in chapters 8 and 9, modelled on the plagues in Egypt when Moses was confronting Pharaoh. Does this show that there are going to be *more* dramatic 'signs' as the prelude to the destruction of the great city, 'Babylon' – normally taken as Rome?

I don't think so. For a start, the book of Revelation (as is well known) is full of fantastic imagery which is certainly not meant to be taken literally as a video-transcript of 'what is going to happen'. There is a sense in which the whole book is simply drawing out the significance of the primary revelation, which is of Jesus himself (1.1–16). The title of the whole book is 'Revelation of Jesus the Messiah' (1.1). It is to Jesus himself – the Lion who is also the Lamb – that the task of taking forwards God's whole project has been entrusted (5.6–14). All that follows in the book, then, is not something *other than* the unveiling of the truth of Jesus. It is, to be sure, applied to the

37

world in various ways. Yet the victory of the Lamb, already won on the cross, is what matters.

The only sense in which that victory might be said to be extended forwards in time is in the suffering and witness of the Lamb's followers. That is explicit in Revelation (6.9; 7.14–17). Jesus' early followers knew that this suffering was not, theologically speaking, something *other than* the one-off sufferings of Jesus himself, and that the witness was actually Jesus himself, by his Spirit, announcing the news through them. This is part of the mystery by which Jesus' disciples understood themselves, indwelt as they were by Jesus' Spirit, to be part of an identity larger than themselves, the messianic reality of Jesus himself. That is why Paul can speak in a dramatic passage in Colossians (1.24) of completing, in his own flesh, what had been lacking in the Messiah's sufferings on behalf of his body. The one-off death of the Messiah is proclaimed, portrayed before the world – sometimes visibly, in the form of the apostle's own suffering. Paul says as much in 2 Corinthians 4 and 6. (This may also be the meaning of a cryptic passage in Galatians 3.1–5, where he talks of Jesus being 'publicly portrayed as crucified'. He is perhaps referring to his own arrival in the Galatian towns in a bedraggled and beaten-up state after having been set upon and stoned.) He was a walking parable of the Gospel of the crucified Messiah.

The Groaning of Creation

All of which leads us to one of the most important passages in our whole quest for understanding how, as followers of Jesus, we should approach the question of the Coronavirus. We stand in awe before the greatest chapter in Paul's greatest letter: Romans 8.

People who know Paul's writings know that Romans 8 is full of faith, hope and love. It begins with the great declaration that 'there is no condemnation for those in the Messiah, Jesus', explaining that God 'condemned sin' in the death of Jesus and gave his people the Spirit as the guarantee of being raised from the dead. It ends with a great shout of praise:

> In all these things we are completely victorious through the one who loved us. I am persuaded, you see, that neither death nor life, nor angels nor rulers, nor the present, nor the future, nor powers, nor height, nor depth nor any other creature will be able to separate us from the love of God in King Jesus our Lord.
>
> (Romans 8.37–39)

This chapter describes a house we all want to live in. If we know anything about Christianity, we know that this – victory over all the dark powers inside us and outside, security in the present age and the age to come, all because of the outpoured love of God in the death of Jesus – this is what it's all about. Yet to get from the beginning to the end of this amazing chapter you have to go through the middle; and in the middle there is a strange passage which we often skip over. Except, perhaps, in times like these, when we are driven back to such passages by our circumstances.

Paul has described how all Jesus' followers, having received God's Spirit, are being led by that Spirit to the 'inheritance' which awaits us. Paul is here explicitly drawing on that central Jewish theme, Exodus and Passover. The children of Israel, liberated from Egypt, were led by God himself through the wilderness to their 'inheritance', the promised land. That wasn't an easy time for them. We don't find our pilgrimage easy, either. Indeed, Paul puts it like this:

> The Spirit gives supporting witness to what our own Spirit is saying, that we are God's children. And if we're children, we are also heirs: heirs of God, and fellow heirs with the Messiah, as long as we suffer with him so that we may also be glorified with him.

Suffering, it seems, is the inevitable path we must tread, even though, as Paul quickly adds, this suffering is small and trivial compared with 'the glory that is going to be unveiled for us'.

Just to be clear once more, the 'inheritance' here is not 'heaven', as many Christians have imagined. The 'glory' has nothing to do with going to heaven and shining like angels. The 'inheritance' is the whole renewed creation, the complete heaven-and-earth reality, renewed from top to bottom, as in Revelation 21, with corruption, death and decay abolished for ever. This is the final move in a longer sequence. In the Old Testament we see an extension of the 'inheritance' from the land God promised to Abraham (Genesis 15) to the whole world which God then promised to David (Psalm 2). The early Christians didn't exchange this for an 'otherworldly' heaven for which we would have to leave 'earth' behind. They saw it as being fulfilled by heaven coming to earth at last, so that, as in some of the glorious biblical promises, the whole earth would be filled with the divine glory, as the waters cover the sea (Psalm 72.19 with Isaiah 11.9 and similar passages).

We cannot of course tell what our transformed physicality will be like in God's new creation. Jesus' risen body had strange properties (coming and going through locked doors, but also eating and drinking and able to touch and be touched), but it didn't shine – though it had done earlier, at the transfiguration. Who knows? That's not important. What is important is that the 'glory' here, as in Psalm 8 where humans are 'crowned with glory and honour', is the long-awaited *rule* of redeemed human beings over God's creation. Paul says exactly that in Romans 5.17, and it meshes with the vocation of the redeemed in Revelation 5.10 and elsewhere.

But what will that 'rule' look like? Here we return to the theme of *the way God wants to run his world*. We still come to that question with mediaeval ideas of a monarch at the head of an army, sweeping all before him; or, perhaps, with eighteenth-century ideas of machines which simply work the way the inventor intended. Either way, we often suppose that God's way of 'controlling' the world is like one or the other, or a mixture of both. A majestic machine. Thus, if something strange happens in the world, we assume that this must be what God intended, or at least what he chose to permit. We then try to draw inferences from this ('if God allowed *this* to happen, it must be because he was trying to tell us something'). Once again, I insist: God can do whatever God wants, and if he chooses on special occasions to do, or permit, certain things for certain purposes, that is entirely his business, not ours. Just because that possibility always remains open, we shouldn't use it as an excuse to escape from the challenge – personal and theological – of this passage, at the heart of the chapter:

Creation itself is on tiptoe with expectation, eagerly awaiting the moment when God's children will be revealed. Creation, you see, was subjected to pointless futility, not of its own volition, but because of the one who placed it in this subjection, in the hope that creation itself would be freed from its slavery to decay, to enjoy the freedom that comes when God's children are glorified.

In other words: God always wanted to rule his world *through* human beings. That is part of what it means to be made in God's image. It was gloriously fulfilled in the human being Jesus; and the way creation will at last become what it was always meant to be will be through the wise, rescuing, restorative rule of renewed, resurrected human beings. All those indwelt by the Spirit are, like Jesus, to be image-bearers, 'shaped according to the model of the image of his son', as Paul puts it in verse 29.

So what does this mean in practice?

It means that, when the world is going through great convulsions, the followers of Jesus are called to be *people of prayer at the place where the world is in pain.* Paul puts it like this, in a three-stage movement: first, the groaning of the world; second, the groaning of the Church; third, the groaning of the Spirit – *within* the Church *within* the world. This is the ultimate answer, I think, to those who want to say that the present Coronavirus crisis is a clear message from God which we can at once decode, either as a sign of the End, a call to repent, or simply an opportunity for a standard kind of evangelism. Here's how Paul expresses it:

We know that the entire creation is groaning together, and going through labour pains together, up until the present time. Not only so: we too, we who have the first fruits of the Spirit's life within us, are groaning within ourselves, as we eagerly await our adoption, the redemption of our body. We were saved, you see, in hope…

In the same way, too, the Spirit comes alongside and helps us in our weakness. We don't know what to pray for as we ought to; but that same Spirit pleads on our behalf, with groanings too deep for words. And the Searcher of Hearts knows what the Spirit is thinking, because the Spirit pleads for God's people according to God's will.

(Romans 8.22–27)

Notice that Paul here says more or less the exact opposite of what some followers of Jesus are wanting to say at this time. Here is the world, groaning in travail: yes, we recognize that picture all right. There hasn't been a moment like this in my lifetime. It is taking its toll not only in many thousands of deaths, but in the stress and distress of millions who are shut in without company or help, or at the mercy of abusive partners, or losing jobs and livelihoods; or simply those whose temperament plunges them into gloom after a few days of being confined to the house. We know all that. So where should the Church be in the middle of it?

As we've seen, some are saying that the Church should be commenting from the sidelines: it's because you're all sinners! It's because the End is near! We know what's going on and we need to tell you! Yet that's not what Paul says. Paul says that the followers of Jesus are caught up in the same 'groaning'. We are painfully aware of a big gap between the people we are right now (weak, frail, muddled, corruptible) and the people we shall be (risen from the dead into a glorious, new and immortal physicality). At the moment this means that we share the groaning of creation. This speaks directly to questions about what the Church itself should be doing at the present time.

The thing above all which the Church should be doing at the present time is *praying*. But this is a strange prayer indeed. Here we are, at the heart of one of the most glorious chapters in Scripture, and here is Paul saying *We don't know what to pray for as we ought*. We are at a loss! He implies that this isn't something we ought to be ashamed of. It is the natural place to be. It is a kind of exile; a kind of fasting; a moment of not-knowing, not being in 'control', not sharing what we might think of as 'glory' at all.

Yet that is the very moment when we are caught up in the inner, Triune life of God. Here is the dark mystery to which our present situation might alert us: the one thing we know from all this is that 'not-knowing' is itself the right place to be. There is a sense in which this is the deeply Christian version of Socrates's principle: he didn't claim to know much, but he knew that he didn't know and so kept asking questions. Translate that up into fully Trinitarian life and this is what you get: at the very moment when we discover that we ourselves are 'groaning' and don't know what to say or do, at that same moment we find that God himself, God the Holy Spirit, is 'groaning' as well, groaning without words.

There is a pattern here. Those who have long pondered the story of Jesus will recognize it. We expect God to be, as we might say, 'in charge': taking control, sorting things out, getting things done. *But the God we see in Jesus is the God who wept at the tomb of his friend.* The God we see in Jesus is the God-the-Spirit who groans without words. The God we see in Jesus is the one who, to demonstrate what his kind of 'being in charge' would look like, did the job of a slave and washed his disciples' feet.

Peter, blustering as ever, knew that this was all wrong. Jesus should be the top dog, and he, Peter would fight for him! (John 13.6–10; 37–38) The Church is always faced with the Petrine temptations: to run the world the 'ordinary' way, if necessary by fighting... but then to collapse in a heap when trouble comes. Instead, what we see of God the Spirit in Romans 8 reminds me inescapably of what we see of God the Son in John 13. As the hymn puts it:

> We strain to glimpse your mercy-seat
> And find you kneeling at our feet.

So what are we saying? Not only do we, the followers of Jesus, not have any words to say, any great pronouncements on 'what this all means' to trumpet out to the world (the world, of course, isn't waiting eagerly to hear us anyway); but we, the followers of Jesus, find ourselves caught up in the groaning of creation, and we discover that at the same time God the Spirit is groaning within us. *That is our vocation: to be in prayer, perhaps wordless prayer, at the point where the world is in pain.* At those very moments when we find ourselves weeping with grief at the death of a friend or family member, or at the impossibility of having a proper funeral, or at the horror of millions of the world's poorest being at risk, or simply because being locked down is inherently depressing – at those moments, when any words we try to say come out as sobs or tears, we have to remind ourselves that this is how God the Spirit is present at the heart of the agony of creation. Yes: just like Jesus himself being hailed as 'king of the Jews' when he shared the agony of Israel and the world on the cross. The redefinition of 'control', of 'kingdom', of 'sovereignty', which we find in the rest of the New Testament and particularly with Jesus himself, here reaches its true depth.

To understand this strange phenomenon – God himself, God the Spirit, apparently unable to manage words, but only groans! – Paul reaches back to that great Psalm of lament, Psalm 44. God is the one who searches the hearts and knows exactly what's going on there. When our hearts are groaning, within the groaning of all creation, the God who searches the hearts – the Father, in other words – knows 'the mind of the Spirit', as some translations put it. He knows what the Spirit is thinking. Here is the mystery. God the Father knows the Spirit's mind; but the mind that the Father thereby knows is the mind that doesn't know what to say.

Dare we then say that God the creator, facing his world in melt-down, is himself in tears, even though he remains the God of ultimate Providence? That would be John's answer, if the story of Jesus at Lazarus's tomb is anything to go by. Might we then say that God the creator, whose Word brought all things into being and pronounced it 'very good', has no appropriate words to say to the misery when creation is out of joint? Paul's answer, from this present passage, seems to point in that direction. The danger with speaking confident words into a world out of joint is that we fit the words to the distortion and so speak distorted words – all to protect a vision of a divinity who cannot be other than 'in control' all the time.

At this point, of course, someone might quote the next verse. Romans 8.28 has often been translated something like, 'All things work together for good to those who love God'. That is the line taken by the King James Version, the NRSV, the ESV, the first marginal option in the NIV, and others. That is what many Christians were brought up to believe, making people think they ought to be able to say, of any and every disaster, that in some way it was 'for the best'. Many who have understood it like that – and who have found, let's be clear, a kind of comfort in it – have effectively skipped over the previous verses. ('They seem rather strange, but God will work it all out!') That has then sometimes cast an almost Stoic blanket over anything 'bad' that happens. 'Never mind, all things work together for good.'

Is that really Christian comfort? Is that kind of passive 'acceptance' really what the verses we have been studying seem to be advocating? Is that the appropriate response to the Coronavirus disaster?

I don't think it is. I have been helped here by certain recent scholars who have argued strongly for an alternative approach which, though occasionally suggested, has never been widely accepted. (See Haley G. Jacob in *Conformed to the Image of his Son* [Downers Grove: IVP Academic, 2018], 245–51; and Sylvia C. Keesmaat and Brian J. Walsh, *Romans Disarmed* [Grand Rapids: Brazos, 2019], 375–379. Their solutions are similar, but not identical, to the proposal of Robert Jewett, *Romans* [Minneapolis: Fortress Press, 2007], 526–528.)

The way forward is to challenge two regular assumptions about the sentence.

First, is 'all things' really the subject of the sentence? Is Paul telling us, in this most God-oriented of chapters, that 'all things' have a kind of internal energy and operation by themselves?

No. It is in fact far more likely that 'God' is the subject. Some early manuscripts added *ho theos*, 'God', to make this clear. God is after all the subject of the previous verse, albeit referred to as 'the Searcher of Hearts'. The Spirit is the subject of the second clause in verse 27 ('because the Spirit pleads for God's people according to God's will), but this point is subordinate to the main sentence, where the main subject is 'the heart-searcher', God himself. It is easiest to assume that this carries on into verse 28. In verse 28 itself, God is twice referred to as 'he' ('those who love *him*' and 'according to *his* purpose'), which implies that he is already present in the sentence-construction. 'God' is then clearly the subject of verses 29 and 30, which follow on immediately.

Some, however, have argued that the Spirit, the subject of verse 26 and mentioned in the second half of verse 27, is the real subject, rather than 'all things' or 'God'. Most scholars, however, have thought this less likely.

Second, and even more important, why are we so sure that verse 28 speaks of God working all things *for the benefit of* those who love him? That is the 'normal' reading offered by the King James and others, and as we have seen it can be made to fit, either with 'all things' working together for good, or with 'God' who is working all things together for good, or indeed with 'the Spirit' as subject. The King James version, taking 'all things' as the subject, renders it 'all things work together for good *to* them that love God'. The NIV main text paraphrases, taking 'God' as the subject and making 'those who love him' the beneficiaries: 'in all things God works for the good *of* those who love him'. I have followed this line in my own translation (*The New Testament for Everyone* / *The Kingdom New Testament*): 'God works all things together for good to those who love him.'

The problem with this is that the verb doesn't mean 'to work *for the benefit of*'; it means 'to work *with*'. The word here isn't the normal word for 'work', *ergazomai* . It is *synergeō*, 'work together'. The *syn-* at the start means 'together' or 'with'; the *erg-* bit means 'work'.

Paul uses this word on two other occasions. In 1 Corinthians 16.16 he's talking about the 'fellow-workers' who collaborate with him and with the whole Church. In 2 Corinthians 6.1 he sums up the previous passage (about God working *through* the apostles, like a monarch acting through his ambassadors), by saying that he is 'working together' with God.

This would imply that if Paul is talking here about God being at work, he is saying that God is working *with* people, doing what he wants to do in the world, not all by himself, but through human agency. This is of course normal in biblical theology, looking back to the image-bearing vocation of humans in Genesis 1 and Psalm 8.

The cognate noun, *synergos*, is more common than the verb. Paul uses it eleven times to refer to his colleagues, people who *work with* him. Once he uses it to say that we – the apostles – are *God's* colleagues, working with him (1 Corinthians 3.9). That seems to be the point here. God works all things towards ultimate good *with and through* those who love him.

You could still get a similar meaning with 'the Spirit' as the subject. That's what Robert Jewett suggests in his commentary. This seems to be the line taken by the NEB and REB: 'and in everything… he [the Spirit] co-operates for good with those who love God'.

But I prefer the suggestion in the NEB margin. This is close to what is now proposed by Jacob, and by Keesmaat and Walsh: 'God himself co-operates for good with those who love God'. This is anticipated in the RSV ('in everything God works for good *with* those who love him'). It is suggested as a second alternative in the margin of the NIV ('in all things God works together with those who love him to bring about what is good'). The Spirit, as in verses 16, 26 and 27, is the one at work within believers, and this Spirit-and-believer combination is the joint unit with which the Father is co-operating. The very moment of the wordless lament described in verse 26 is the moment when God the Father and God the Spirit are working together, with believers caught up by the Spirit within that strange but vital interchange.

So the encouragement and comfort here in Romans 8.28 doesn't amount to a kind of Stoic resignation. It is a call to recognise the truth of what Paul says elsewhere: that we are called to hard work, knowing that God is at work in us. That work, it seems, takes place not least through suffering with the Messiah in order to share his 'image-bearing' human 'glory' (8.17, 29). When Paul speaks here of believers as 'those who love God', he seems to be reflecting the heart-to-heart communication, consisting of a lament too deep for words, which he has just described.

The last phrase of the verse ('who are called according to his purpose') then seems to be describing, not God's purpose *for* these people – that he would give them final salvation – but his purpose *through* these people. God has 'called' them to be part of his saving purpose for his suffering world. Believers, at this point, may not have words to speak their lament. But they may still have work to do, in healing, teaching, poor relief, campaigning and comforting. These things grow out of lament. As with the church in Antioch, we may not be able to say 'Why', but we may glimpse 'What': Who is at risk? What can be done? Who shall we send? Ironically, it has been easy in some traditions to reverse this: to be afraid of adding 'works', lest one might compromise grace and faith, but to be only too ready to add explanatory words where, as Paul insists, even the Spirit remains inarticulate.

Paul is not, then, proposing a Christian version of Stoicism. He is offering a Jesus-shaped picture of a suffering, redeeming providence, in which God's people are themselves not simply spectators, not simply beneficiaries, but active participants. They are 'called according to his purpose', since God is even now using their groaning, at the heart of the world's pain, as the vehicle for the Spirit's own work, holding that sorrow before the Father, creating a context for the multiple works of healing and hope. Such God-lovers are therefore shaped according to the pattern of the Son: the cruciform pattern in which God's justice and mercy, his faithfulness to the covenant and to creation, are displayed before the world in tears and toil, lament and labour.

That is our vocation in the present time.

5

Where Do We Go from Here?

Why Must We Lament?

I have urged that we should embrace lament as the vital initial Christian response to this pandemic. Roughly one-third of the Psalms are lamenting that things are not as they should be. The words they use are words of complaint: of question, sorrow, anger and frustration and, often enough, bitterness. They are all part of the prayer-book of Jesus himself, and the New Testament draws freely on them to express not only our own laments but the way of Jesus too.

The Lord's Prayer is our 'norm'. Are we looking for sudden signs of the End? No: we pray every day, 'Thy Kingdom Come on earth as in heaven', and we know that prayer will be answered because of what we know about Jesus. Are we looking for fresh, sudden calls to repent? No: we pray every day, 'Forgive us our Trespasses, as we forgive those who trespass against us.' We know *that* prayer will be answered, because of what we know about Jesus.

Are we then looking for fresh reasons to leave our comfortable lifestyles and tell our neighbours the good news? Well, shame on us if it takes a pandemic to get us to that point. Why wasn't Jesus' command enough? 'As the father sent me, so I'm sending you'; 'Go and make all nations into disciples'. As Paul knew in Athens, you don't need extra signs. More is less, as so often. You need Jesus: his kingdom-bringing life, death and resurrection; his ascended sovereignty; the promise of his coming to bring heaven and earth together in glorious final renewal. Every attempt to add new 'signs' to this narrative diminishes it. It implies that, in Jesus' parable of the vineyard tenants, the owner did after all have a few more messengers he could send, even after sending his only son and watching him be rejected and killed.

In a time of acute crisis, when death sneaks into houses and shops, when you may feel healthy yourself but you may be carrying the virus without knowing it, when every stranger on the street is a threat, when we go around in masks, when churches are shut and people are dying with nobody to pray by their bedside – this is a time for lament. For admitting we don't have easy answers. For refusing to use the crisis as a loudspeaker for what we'd been wanting to say in any case. For weeping at the tomb of our friends. For the inarticulate groaning of the Spirit. 'Rejoice with those who rejoice,' said Paul, 'and weep with those who weep.' Yes, and the world is weeping right now. The initial calling of the Church, first and foremost, is to take our place humbly among the mourners.

Grief, after all, is part of love. Not to grieve, not to lament, is to slam the door on the same place in the innermost heart from which love itself comes. Our culture is afraid of grief, but not just because it is afraid of death. That is natural and normal, a proper reaction to the Last Enemy. Our culture is afraid because it seems to be afraid of the fear itself, frightened that even to name grief will be to collapse for ever. We have to keep going, we tell ourselves, we have to be strong. Well, yes. Strong like Jesus who wept at the tomb of his friend. Strong like the Spirit who raised Jesus from the dead and will give life to our mortal bodies too – but who, right now, is pleading for us with groanings too deep for words. Strong like the person who learns to pray the Psalms. Strong like the person who learns to wait patiently for the Lord, and expects neither easy answers nor easy words to say to the world:

I said to my soul, be still, and let the dark come upon you
Which shall be the darkness of God...
I said to my soul, be still, and wait without hope,
For hope would be hope for the wrong thing; wait without
    love
For love would be love of the wrong thing; there is yet faith
But the faith and the hope and the love are all in the
    waiting.
Wait without thought, for you are not yet ready for
    thought:
So the darkness shall be the light, and the stillness the
    dancing...
In order to arrive at what you do not know
You must go by a way which is the way of ignorance...

So mused T. S. Eliot in *East Coker*, the second of the *Four Quartets*, written when the skies over London were dark with German warplanes. Eliot had realized that all the easy comforts for which we reach when things are tough are likely to be delusions. We grab at them – and perhaps we hope that God will quickly give them to us – so that we don't have to face the darkness. So that we don't have to 'watch and pray' with Jesus in Gethsemane. There is a time for restraint, for fasting, for a sense of exile, of not-belonging. Of defamiliarization. A time for not rushing to judgments. It is all too easy to grasp at quick-fix solutions, in prayer as in life. It can be hard, bitter anguish to live with the summons to lament. To share in the groaning of the Spirit. But that is where we are conformed to the image of the Son.

How Do We Talk about God?

I have argued that it is only with Jesus himself, and with the Spirit, that we really see and know what it means to say that God is 'in control' of his world. Jesus redefined God's kingdom around his own vocation, the climax of which was to be his crucifixion, 'for our sins, in accordance with the scriptures' (1 Corinthians 15.3). He understood the whole narrative of Israel, itself the focal point of the Creator's rescuing purpose for his world, as being funnelled down on to one point, the lonely agony of Good Friday. Jesus had to go into the darkness and take its full weight upon himself. He did so in the belief that this was what it would mean for the ancient promises to be fulfilled, for Israel's God himself to come back in person to accomplish the Ultimate Passover. This would be the way to overthrow the dark cosmic powers. This would be how to rescue the world from death itself and all that causes it.

In doing this, and believing this, Jesus was thoroughly in tune with the vocation of human beings in Genesis: to reflect God's purposes in the world. When humans sinned, God didn't cancel that part of the creational package. He called a human family – knowing full well that they were as flawed as the rest – to be his partners in the work of redemption and new creation. This human family, the people of Abraham, of Moses, of David, arrived at its destiny with Jesus himself, the Jesus who wept at the tomb of his friend, who agonized in Gethsemane, who cried out on the cross that he had been abandoned. That is how God's kingdom was established.

That remains its character. You see that in the Sermon on the Mount. You see it in Acts, when Jesus' followers go out to proclaim that he is already the world's true Lord. Modern rationalists – including modern Christian rationalists, brought up to suppose that rationalist scepticism must be answered by rationalistic apologetics – easily imagine that you solve the problems of the world by sending in the tanks or the bombs. That's what the Western powers have done again and again at the political level. It's what some apologists try to do on the intellectual level: 'God is sovereign; he can do what he likes; therefore whatever happens must be what God wanted, so we must be able to say why.' That wasn't how God established his kingdom, and it isn't how that kingdom now works. Think again of the Antioch church sending help to Jerusalem.

Many things, after all, actually bring grief to God. They shock him. Providence is Jesus-shaped: it isn't an iron grip, relentlessly 'controlling' everything. In Genesis 6.6 God sees the wickedness of humans, and he doesn't say, 'Well, I have allowed that in order to do something with it'; *it grieved him to his heart*. The Hebrew text is explicit on that point. This clearly troubled some later Jewish thinkers, because the Septuagint translation (roughly second century BC) simply says 'and he thought it over'. Anyway, out of that heart-grief God called Noah, through whom God would make a way through the disaster. Yet there is a straight line from what Genesis 6.6 says about God to what Mark 14.33 says about Jesus: 'My soul is disturbed within me, right to the point of death' (quoting Psalms 42 and 43, two classic 'laments'). John has Jesus say much the same thing: 'Now my heart is troubled' (12.27, quoting Psalm 6). Jesus can see the flood of death and despair coming upon him. Unlike Noah, he will have no Ark.

Nevertheless, he will take with him God's whole creation, through the flood of death and out into the new creation that dawns on Easter morning.

Equally, some things apparently shock God. The Israelites were told again and again that they should not practice human sacrifice. However, they didn't simply do it on the sly; they constructed great 'high places' for this specific purpose. God's response is to say, I didn't command this, *nor did it come into my mind* (Jeremiah 7.31; repeated in 32.35). Actually, the Hebrew text again says 'heart' both times. God neither intended it nor even dreamed of it.

That is of course a paradox. We see it most sharply when Peter says to the crowd in Acts 2.23 that the death of Jesus was what God had intended and planned – but that the people who arrested, tried and killed him were wicked to do so. There is no way round this paradox, nor should we look for one. We are not given nice, comprehensible, mechanistic analyses. Evil is an intruder into God's creation. Any attempt to analyse either what it is, why it's allowed or what God does with it – apart from the clear, strong statement that God overcomes it through Jesus' death for sinners – is not only trying to put the wind into a bottle; it is supposing that we can imagine an orderly universe in which 'evil' has an appropriate, allowable place.

That way danger lies: to give an account of God's good creation in which there is a 'natural' slot for 'evil' to be found. The old philosophers' 'problem of evil' cannot be 'solved' except at the foot of the cross; just as the politicians' 'problem of evil' (such as emerged after 9/11 when George Bush and Tony Blair talked grandly of there being an 'axis of evil' which they were going to deal with) is always a dangerous way to go about things. Bush and Blair thought that the way to solve their 'problem of evil' was by dropping bombs from a great height. Every one of those bombs, as some people predicted at the time, turned out to be another recruiting agent for yet more extreme forms of radical Islamism. In the same way, the rationalistic analyses of 'evil' offered by some ('God allowed the Holocaust to create an opportunity for some people to develop the virtues of heroism, self-sacrifice and so on' – or perhaps 'God allowed the Holocaust in order that the modern State of Israel would arise') serve as recruiting agents for new forms of radical atheism. They would offer the dark, disturbing picture of a god who deliberately allowed a dangerous virus to escape from a Chinese laboratory or market in order that, by killing millions of innocent people, God could issue a general call to repentance to those who were left, and create a stage on which some people (the doctors and nurses) could develop and display heroism. If that's your 'god', many of our contemporaries would rightly think, don't expect us to want anything to do with him.

It is altogether more appropriate, then, to recognize that God has in fact delegated the running of many aspects of his world to human beings. In doing so, he has run the risk that they will grieve him to his heart or shock him out of his mind. But when this happens, he will hold people responsible. That is the other side of the coin of his delegation of authority to his image-bearers. After all, Jesus recognizes that Pontius Pilate has a genuine, God-delegated authority over him. He merely comments that God will therefore hold to account those responsible for handing him over (John 19.11). This is why we need proper investigation and accountability for whatever it was that caused the virus to leak out, and for the lesser ways in which various countries and governments have, or have not, dealt wisely in preparing for a pandemic and then handling it when it rushed upon us.

All that brings us to the question: how do we live with this problem, and how do we come through it? What – as well as lament – is the calling of the Church in the midst of it?

How Do We Live in the Present?

The Church's mission began (according to John 20) with three things which have become very familiar to us in recent days. It began with tears; with locked doors; and with doubt.

On the first Easter day, Mary Magdalene was weeping in the garden outside Jesus' empty tomb (John 20.1–18). To her astonishment, Jesus met her, spoke to her – and gave her a commission. She was to go and tell the disciples, who were in hiding. that he was alive, and that he was now to be enthroned as Lord of the world.

That same evening the disciples were still in hiding, with the doors locked (John 20.19–23). They were naturally afraid that the people who had come after Jesus would soon be coming come after them too. But the locked doors didn't stop Jesus. He came and stood with them. He shared a meal with them. He gave them their mission: 'As the father has sent me,' he said, 'so I'm sending you.' What did that mean? The most obvious way of taking it, as we'll see below, is to say, As Jesus was to Israel, so the Church is to the world.

The next week the disciples were in the same room, locked in once more. Thomas hadn't been there the first time. He had spent the week telling the others he'd never believe it until Jesus showed up and proved it was really him (John 20.24–29). Jesus came again, and invited Thomas to touch and see the wounds in his hands and his side: the scars which proved his identity, the wounds that revealed his love.

Tears, locked doors and doubt seem to go together. Different ways of saying similar things. Together they sum up a lot of where we are globally at the time I'm writing this. Tears in plenty, of course: so many lives cut short. Locked doors: well, precisely. The fear isn't just of certain people who may have it in for us; it's a larger, more nebulous fear that every stranger in the street might, without knowing it, give me a sickness which could kill me within a week. I might be able to give it to them, as well. So: lockdown. And, like a weed growing between the weeping and the lock-down, there is doubt: what's this all about? Is there any room left for faith, for hope? If we are locked away from all but a few, any room for love? These are hard and pressing questions.

They are the kind of questions the Church ought to be good at answering. At answering not just verbally (who's listening, anyway?), but symbolically.

If the earliest disciples found Jesus coming to meet them in their tears, fears and doubt, perhaps we can too.

But how?

What, in particular, might it mean to say that 'as Jesus was to Israel, so the Church should be for the world'?

As we saw earlier, John's Gospel displays the *signs* that Jesus was doing. These were not things like earthquakes or famines, plagues or floods. They were not meant to frighten people into submission or belief, or to warn them that the world was coming to a shuddering halt. They were signs of new life, of new creation. They were signs of God coming into the ordinary and making it extraordinary. Coming to bring healing to a world of sickness. Giving bread to the hungry; sight to the blind; life to the dead. They were signs that the world was coming into a new springtime. A new beginning.

In the upper room, Jesus was commissioning his tearful, fearful, doubting followers to do the same.

And so they did. Right from the start. In Paul's very first letter he tells the Galatians to 'do good to all people, especially those of the household of faith.'

The outside world couldn't believe it. As we saw, when faced with a plague, the early Christians would pitch in and nurse people, sometimes saving lives, sometimes dying themselves. Their strong belief in God's promises for life beyond the grave gave them a fearlessness which enabled them both to keep cheerful in the face of death and to go to the aid of sufferers whose own families and communities had abandoned them for fear of the disease.

This is well set out in Rodney Stark's famous book *The Rise of Christianity* (1996, Ch. 4). Stark makes a compelling case that the way the Christians behaved in the great plagues of the early centuries was a significant factor in contributing to the spread of the faith. Stark, and others who have followed him, have collected the evidence from the plagues of the 170s AD, which killed the Emperor Marcus Aurelius, and the 250s. (Nobody is quite sure what diseases they were. One might have been smallpox, the other measles, both killers when attacking unprepared populations.) The emperor Julian, who tried to de-convert the Roman empire in the late fourth century after it had become officially Christian under Constantine, complained that the Christians were much better at looking after the sick, and for that matter the poor, than the ordinary non-Christian population. He was trying to lock the stable door after the horse had bolted. The Christians were being for the world what

Jesus had been for Israel. People took notice. Something new was happening.

The tradition continued. It was the Christians who built hospitals and hospices. The followers of Jesus were first in the field, too, in making education available outside the circles of the elite, and in the care of the poor. All were needed, as they still are. As for medicine, it's only in the very modern period that there has been something of a lull in major epidemics, as germs became identified and understood, and vaccination and other preventative measures became the norm. So from the time of Jesus until the last century or two, plagues and the like have continued to come and go, often with terrifying consequences. If we thought that because we now lived in the 'modern world' we were exempt – that our science and technology had now produced 'progress' that would eliminate all such things – we were obviously wrong. Just like those at the end of the nineteenth century who thought that Western society was now advancing smoothly towards the Kingdom of God.

So, throughout Church history, Jesus' followers have usually avoided such lines of thought. Instead, like the church in Antioch, they have got on with the job. They have visited the prisoners, cared for the wounded, welcomed the strangers, fed the hungry. And they have tended the sick. In most past ages that has been done day and night, in good times and bad, in the Black Death and the Bubonic Plague, in war and peace, in the slums of the city and the isolated farmhouses. Clergy and laity alike have done it, at considerable and often fatal risk to themselves. The urge to meet the Lord himself in the faces of the needy – in accordance with Matthew 25 – has always been strong.

When the present pandemic began to take hold, a passage from the writings of Martin Luther went the rounds on the internet, with Luther's usual combination of down-to-earth wisdom and practical piety. Luther faced several plagues in Wittenberg and elsewhere in the 1520s and 1530s, and in his letters to church and civic leaders he insisted that preachers and pastors should remain at their posts: as good shepherds, they should be prepared to lay down their lives for their sheep. Likewise civic and family leaders should only flee from a plague if they had made proper provision for the safety of those left behind. He offers advice which sounds as relevant today as it was five hundred years ago. Plagues, he says, may perhaps be messengers from God; but the right approach should be practical as well as faithful. This, he says, is how one should think to oneself:

> With God's permission the enemy has sent poison and deadly dung among us, and so I will pray to God that he may be gracious and preserve us. Then I will fumigate to purify the air, give and take medicine, and avoid places and persons where I am not needed in order that I may not abuse myself and that through me others may not be infected and inflamed with the result that I become the cause of their death through my negligence. If God wishes to take me, he will be able to find me. At least I have done what he gave me to do and am responsible neither for my own death nor for the death of others. But if my neighbour needs me, I shall avoid neither person nor place but feel free to visit and help him.
>
> *Luther: Letters of Spiritual Counsel*, ed. T. G. Tappert
> (London: SCM Press, 1955), 242, from a letter of 1527.

There is a gritty wisdom at the heart of this. Luther clearly believed that the 'normal' course of action was for a Christian to stay and help, rather than run away, when a plague strikes a district. Yet he knew, even in the days before people understood how germs and viruses worked, that it was quite possible for a well-meaning person to make matters worse. We today know that only too well: someone may carry, and transmit, the Covid-19 virus without knowing they have it. So the natural inclination of a Jesus-follower, to obey Jesus' call to go and help at the place of danger, even at the risk of one's own life, looks rather different when that apparently heroic action might easily make matters worse. The generous one-dimensional desire to be a hero, to 'do the right thing', needs to be rounded out with the equally generous willingness to restrain apparent heroism when it might itself bring disaster.

Yet this cannot become an excuse for doing nothing. Out of lament must come fresh action. At the very least, clergy (properly trained, authorized and protectively clothed) must be allowed to attend the sick and dying. If, as sometimes seems to be the case, secular doctors suppose that such ministry is superfluous, this must be challenged at every level. As we thank God that in the last two or three centuries the long-term calling of the Church to bring healing and hope has been shared in the wider secular world, we must work with the medical profession, not least to ensure a fully rounded, fully human approach. This applies particularly when people are near the point of death; the hospice movement of the last fifty years has been largely a Christian innovation, privately funded, witnessing to a hope that secular medicine has sometimes ignored.

The call to Jesus' followers, then, as they confront their own doubts and those of the world through tears and from behind locked doors, is to be sign-producers for God's kingdom.

We are to set up signposts – actions, symbols, not just words – which speak, like Jesus' signs, of new creation: of healing for the sick, of food for the hungry, and so on. This means things like running food banks, working in homeless shelters, volunteering to help those visiting relatives in prisons, and so on. These can be rewarding tasks but they, and all similar things, are also demanding. For them we will need, as Mary, Thomas and the disciples in the upper room needed, the living presence of Jesus, and the powerful breath of his Spirit. That is what we are promised.

In following this vocation, we will thereby be doing what Jesus told his followers in John 16: in the power of the Spirit, we will be holding the world to account. Just as the Jesus-followers were showing the officials of the Roman empire that there was a different way to run society, so there will be signs of God's kingdom that can emerge from the creative, healing, restorative work of church members today. Situations and opportunities will vary, but out of the lament of God's people new possibilities can and do emerge. As Jesus' followers today grieve in prayer at the heart of the world's pain, new vocations may emerge, both of healing and wisdom and of holding up a mirror to those in power to show what has needed to be done.

Of course, once you have a major National Health Service, as we do in Britain, the inclination is to suppose that the State now runs 'health' and the churches can go back to being 'spiritual', to teaching people to pray and showing them how to get to 'heaven'. Ever since the eighteenth century the 'secular' world has done its best to take over, and to claim the credit for, a great deal that the Jesus-followers used to do. The Church has often gone along for the ride, sliding off into a Platonic rejection of 'the world' and offering an escapist 'evangelism' and 'spirituality'. Yet when government funding is cut, and the health services can no longer do what they need to, churches should be the ones – but often are not – to raise their voices in protest and to step in and help. We have a long track record on medical work, much longer than any other society or company. Suddenly to be told that we cannot and must not do it, but must leave it to 'the professionals', feels like being told that we cannot and must not be the Church. Others claim to know best (though actually the scientific advice is worryingly diverse) and we aren't wanted on the patch. We should not be afraid to take the high ground. This is part of the work of holding the world to account in the power of the Spirit.

This raises the current controversy over whether church buildings should be locked, and services held over the internet from people's homes. Here there seem to me to be two quite different things which need to be said (as often happens in Christian theology). We need to hear them both.

First, church buildings are not an escape from the world, but a bridgehead into the world. A proper theology of 'sacred space' ought to see buildings for public worship as advance signs of the time when God's glory will fill all creation. (I have developed this idea further in *Interpreting Scripture* (2020, Ch. 18).) We should therefore celebrate every way in which the living Lord whom we regularly worship in church buildings is out and about, bringing healing and hope far beyond the visible limits of church property.

The poet Malcolm Guite has caught this brilliantly, reflecting on this last Easter with churches locked, and on the recent British innovation of people coming out of their houses on Thursday evenings to applaud our courageous health workers. I am grateful to Malcolm for permission to quote the whole piece:

Easter 2020

And where is Jesus, this strange Easter day?
　Not lost in our locked churches, anymore
　Than he was sealed in that dark sepulchre.
The locks are loosed; the stone is rolled away,
　And he is up and risen, long before,
　Alive, at large, and making his strong way
　Into the world he gave his life to save,
　No need to seek him in his empty grave.

　He might have been a wafer in the hands
　Of priests this day, or music from the lips:
　Of red-robed choristers, instead he slips
Away from church, shakes off our linen bands
　To don his apron with a nurse: he grips
And lifts a stretcher, soothes with gentle hands
　The frail flesh of the dying, gives them hope,
Breathes with the breathless, lends them strength to cope.

　On Thursday we applauded, for he came
　And served us in a thousand names and faces
Mopping our sickroom floors and catching traces
　Of that *corona* which was death to him:
　Good Friday happened in a thousand places
Where Jesus held the helpless, died with them
　That they might share his Easter in their need,
　Now they are risen with him, risen indeed.

As in all Malcolm Guite's work, there is a deep wisdom here. Jesus does not need church buildings for his work to go forward. Part of the answer to the question, 'Where is God in the pandemic?' must be, 'Out there on the front line, suffering and dying to bring healing and hope.'

However, there is a second point which has to be made. In those countries such as my own where churches (and other places of worship, including synagogues and mosques) have been shut, for thoroughly comprehensible reasons, there is a danger of accidentally sending the wrong signal to the wider world. For the last three hundred years the western world has regarded 'religion' (the very word has changed its meaning to accommodate this new viewpoint) as a private matter: 'what someone does with their solitude'. The Christian faith as a whole has been reduced, in the public mind, to a 'private' movement in the sense that – so many say – it should have no place in public life. Thus I can still go shopping in the crowded little off-licence (in America, the liquor store) on the corner; but I cannot go and sit in the ancient, prayer-soaked chapel across the street. Worship becomes invisible. Shutting churches will appear to collude with this. By saying that we will temporarily abolish corporate worship and join with others only on live-streamed services from the vicar's living room, we may seem to be agreeing that really we are just a group of like-minded individuals pursuing our rather arcane private hobby. The danger with e-worship is that it can turn into P-worship – the Platonic vision of 'the flight of the alone to the alone'. Since there are cultural pressures in that direction already, it's important that we should recognise the danger.

Happily, the signs so far are that many people have 'been to church' in that virtual reality who would not have come to a church building, so that is an exciting development. Yet our churches have been for centuries physical and often audible reminders, on high streets and in city squares, on village greens and in suburban developments, of the vital dimension to life which Western modernity has tried to crowd out. We will no doubt learn many things in this time of enforced 'exile' – which is what it is – but we should be praying towards the day when our buildings will function within our society as they were designed to do.

In other words, I am concerned with the ways in which the Church, faced with a major crisis, has meekly followed what seems to be a secularizing lead. *The sign of new creation, from the ministry of Jesus forward, has been the healing presence of Jesus himself, and his death and resurrection above all.* Public worship of the Triune God, in a public place – observing whatever security measures are appropriate – has always been a major part of sending out that signal to the watching world. When Paul tells the Philippians to 'Rejoice in the Lord always', the word 'rejoice' doesn't just mean 'feel very happy deep inside'. It means, Get out on the street (with proper safe distancing of course) and celebrate! Lots of other people are doing it, after all – in Paul's day, there were processions and street parties and religious ceremonies going on a lot, in public, and people could see what was happening. Paul wanted the Jesus-followers to do the same. In the Bible the word 'joy' signifies something you can *hear*. From some distance away; check out Nehemiah 12.43.

I find myself caught between these two viewpoints, both of which seem to me right. I totally understand that we need to be responsible and scrupulously careful. I am appalled by reports of would-be devout but misguided people ignoring

safety regulations because they believe that as Christians
they are automatically protected against disease, or that
(as I heard someone say on television) 'you'll be safe inside
church because the devil can't get in there'. (I wanted
to say: Trust me, lady, I'm a bishop: the devil knows his
way in there as well as anybody else.) That is the kind of
superstition that gets Christian faith a bad name. Equally,
the debates about locking churches can easily stir up lesser
controversies, between those for whom the building and all
its bits and pieces has been a vital part of their spirituality,
and those for whom all such things are irrelevant since one
can worship God anywhere. Both sides here may learn from
the present crisis, and we do well to hold one another in
charitable prayer.

Part of the answer to that prayer, as many have seen,
might be to recognize the present moment as a time of *exile*.
We find ourselves 'by the waters of Babylon', thoroughly
confused and grieving for the loss of our normal life. 'How
can we sing the Lord's song in a strange land?', as in Psalm
137, translates quite easily into 'How can I know the joy of
the Eucharist sitting in front of a computer?' Or 'How can
I celebrate Ascension or Pentecost without being with my
brothers and sisters?'

Of course, part of the point of Psalm 137 is precisely that this
Psalm is itself a 'song of the Lord'. That is the irony: writing a
poem about being unable to write a poem. Part of the discipline
of lament might then be to turn the Lament itself into a song of
sorrow. Perhaps that is part of the way in which we are being
called right now to be people of lament – lamenting even the
fact that we can't lament in the way we would normally prefer.
We need to explore those questions, and the new disciplines

they may demand, in whatever ways we can. Perhaps this, too, is simply to be accepted as part of what life in Babylon is like. We must, as Jeremiah said, settle down into this regime and 'seek the welfare of the city' where we are. Yet let's not pretend it's where we want to be. Let's not forget Jerusalem. Let's not decide to stay here.

This is where the churches (and other groups such as Jewish leaders and thinkers) urgently need to think and pray through what can and should be said, and how to say it in such a way that the leaders of the western world can hear it and act wisely. For this, we move to the final section of this chapter.

How Do We Recover?

Perhaps the most vital question of all, and one which should be near the top of serious conversations at the highest level between Church, state and all interested parties, is how we move back towards whatever the 'new normal' is going to be. Some people have expressed the pious hope that when this is all over we will have a kinder, gentler society. We shall pay our nurses much more. We shall be prepared to give more in taxes to support health services, and we shall give much more help to the hospice movement. We shall have enjoyed the fresh air so much, unpolluted by thousands of cars and planes, that we will want to travel less, and spend more time with family and neighbours. We shall celebrate our emergency services, our delivery companies, and all the people who have looked after us.

I wish I thought this were true. I fear, however, that as soon as restrictions are lifted there will be a rush to start up again such businesses as we can – and, in all sorts of ways, that is quite right and proper. Nobody who is desperate to avoid bankruptcy is going to think twice about using the car again, or the plane, if it will help. We are told on all sides that the economic effects of the lockdown are already catastrophic and could get worse. The problem is then quite like the tragic decisions which leaders face during a war: think of Churchill during the Blitz, deciding whether to sacrifice *that* unit for the sake of rescuing *this* one, and whether to send coded messages to the enemy which will make them bomb *those* houses instead of *these* public buildings. At the time of writing we have been concentrating entirely on 'staying safe' – at a massive cost in terms of bankruptcies, unemployment and social malaise. The huge government handouts to those in need as a result will, sooner or later, have to be paid for. Certainly if the debate is conducted between those who see death as the worst of all possible results and those who see economic ruin as the worst of all possible results the end product is likely to be an acrimonious dialogue of the deaf.

As in the ancient pagan world, a plague makes people say, Which gods are angry? And how can we appease them? As today's secularism is more and more revealing its pagan subtexts, it is fascinating to imagine our present dilemma as a clash between Asclepius, the god of healing, and Mammon, the money-god. Mammon, of course, regularly demands human sacrifices; that is why the poorest of the poor are most at risk in the present medical emergency. Perhaps it's no bad thing for Asclepius to have his turn, though Mars, the god of war, and Aphrodite, the goddess of erotic love, are never far away. Certainly it won't do to cut back on the imperative to healing, just because we hear our favourite god Mammon calling to us from the other corner, looking forward to more of those human sacrifices.

Where Do We Go from Here?

If all this is approached purely pragmatically, as though the machinery of state were, well, machinery, rather than the wise working interrelationship of fully alive human beings, the result will be predictable. The weak will go to the wall again. They usually do. After the 2008 financial crisis, the banks and the big businesses, having accepted huge public bail-out money, quickly got back into their old ways, while the poorest parts of Britain just got poorer and stayed that way. Someone needs to stand up and read – perhaps not the riot act, but Psalm 72. This is the list of priorities that the Church should be articulating, not just in speech but in practical proposals to go at the top of the agenda:

> Give the king your justice, O God, and your
>   righteousness to a king's son…
> May the mountains yield prosperity for the people, and
>   the hills, in righteousness.
> May he defend the cause of the poor of the people,
> give deliverance to the needy, and crush the oppressor…
>
> [The righteous ruler] delivers the needy when they call,
>   the poor and those who have no helper.
> He has pity on the weak and the needy, and saves the
>   lives of the needy.
> From oppression and violence he redeems their life,
> And precious is their blood in his sight.
>
> (Psalm 72.1–4, 12–14)

This too could be mocked as wishful thinking. But it is what the Church at its best has always believed and taught, and what the Church on the front lines has always practised. In the early days of the Church, the Roman emperors and local governors didn't know much about what Christianity really was. Yet they knew this strange movement had people called 'bishops' who were always banging on about the needs of the poor. Wouldn't it be nice if people today had the same impression?

So what does that mean in a world where some of us find being locked down a minor nuisance while others are still crowded in refugee camps or in third-world cities where 'social distancing' is about as easy as flying to the moon? We need to think globally and act locally – but, in doing both, to work with Church leaders from around the world to find policies that will prevent a mad rush back to profiteering with the devil taking the hindmost. Of course, in the middle of that, we need to strengthen the World Health Organization and insist that all countries of the world stick firmly to its policies and protocols. There are, no doubt, big questions to be asked of some of the world's superpowers who have used the current crisis as an occasion for grandstanding or other political game-playing. The electronic rumour mills and the 'fake news' channels have been working overtime as well.

In all this, I return to the theme of Lament. It is perhaps no accident that Psalm 72, setting out the messianic agenda which puts the poor and needy at the top of the list, is followed immediately by Psalm 73, which complains that the rich and powerful are getting it their own way as usual. Perhaps that is how we are bound to live: glimpsing what ought to be, then struggling with the way things actually are. However, the only way to live with that is to *pray* with that; to hold the vision and the reality side by side as we groan with the groaning of all creation, and as the Spirit groans within us so that the new creation may come to birth. What we need right now is someone to do in this challenging moment what Joseph did at Pharaoh's court, analysing the situation and sketching a vision for how to address it. We urgently need statesmanlike, wise leadership, with prayerful Christian leaders taking a place alongside others, to think with both vision and realism through the challenges that we shall face in the coming months. It could be that in the days to come we will see signs of genuine new possibilities, new ways of working which will regenerate old systems and invent new and better ones, which we could then recognize as forward-looking hints of new creation. Or perhaps we will just go back to 'business as usual' in the sense of the same old squabbles, the same old shallow analyses and solutions.

If we simply sit and wait to see, and wring our hands either because our churches are locked, or our golf clubs are shut, or our businesses have been put on hold, then it is all the more likely that the usual forces will take control. Mammon is a very powerful deity. Our leaders know what it takes to appease him. If that fails there is always Mars, the god of war. May the Lord save us from his clutches. If we are to escape those dark forces, we must be alert to the dangers and actively, prayerfully taking other initiatives. The garden is far less likely to grow weeds if we have been planting flowers.

It isn't for me to tell Church leaders, let alone leaders of other faith communities, how they ought to be planning for the coming months, what they ought to be pressing upon our governments. Yet those of us who watch and wait and pray for our leaders in Church and state must use this time of lament as a time of prayer and hope. What we hope for includes the wise human leadership and initiative which will, like that of Joseph in Egypt, bring about fresh and healing policies and actions across God's wide and wounded world:

God and the Pandemic

O send out your light and your truth; let them lead me
Let them bring me to your holy hill and to your dwelling.
Then I will go to the altar of God, to God my exceeding
    joy;
And I will praise you with the harp, O God, my God.
Why are you cast down, O my soul, and why are you
    disquieted within me?
Hope in God; for I shall again praise him, my help and
    my God.

(Psalm 43.3–5)

The New Testament in Its World

An Introduction to the History, Literature, and Theology of the First Christians

N. T. Wright and Michael F. Bird

The New Testament in Its World is your passageway from the twenty-first century to the era of Jesus and the first Christians. In short, it brings together decades of ground-breaking research, writing, and teaching into one volume that will open your eyes to the larger world of the New Testament. It presents the New Testament books as historical, literary, and social phenomena located in the world of Second Temple Judaism, amidst Greco-Roman politics and culture, and within early Christianity. Book, workbook, and video/audio resources are available.

The New Testament in Its World Workbook

ISBN 9780310528708 (softcover)

This resource follows the textbook's structure, offering assessment questions, exercises, and activities to support the students' learning experience.

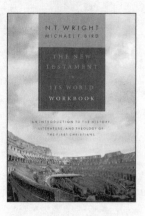

The New Testament in Its World Video Lectures

ISBN 9780310528753 (DVD)
ISBN 9780310528760 (download)

Ideal for enhancing your learning, these 37 lectures were filmed around the world and in-studio. Locations include Jerusalem, Corinth, Athens, Rome, Nazareth, Qumran, Capernaum, and the shores of the Sea of Galilee.

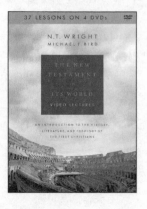

The New Testament in Its World Audio Lectures

ISBN 9780310101819 (Part 1, download)
ISBN 9780310101826 (Part 2, download)

Take the lectures on the go! Professors Wright and Bird will guide you through how to read the New Testament, the world of Jesus and the early church, deep studies on both Jesus and the apostle Paul, and much more.

Collected Essays of N. T. Wright

N. T. Wright

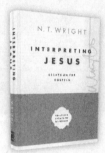  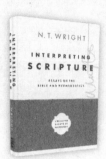

Collected Essays of N. T. Wright brings together N. T. Wright's most important articles on Scripture and hermeneutics, Jesus and the Gospels, and Paul and his letters over the last three decades. Here is a rich feast for all serious students of the New Testament. Each essay in this three-volume collection will amply reward those looking for detailed, incisive, and exquisitely nuanced exegesis, resulting in a clearer, deeper, and more informed appreciation of Scripture and its application to Christian life and thought today. Volumes are available individually or in a set.

Available in stores and online!